Taxes Without Borders

The American Expat's Guide to FEIE, FBAR, Foreign Tax Credits, and Minimizing Your US Tax Bill While Living Abroad

Patricia M. Ashworth

Published by NobleTrex Press

For permissions and other inquiries, write to:

P.O. Box 3132, Framingham, MA 01701, USA

Contents

Introduction

Picture this: You are sitting in a sun-drenched plaza in Madrid, or perhaps looking out over the neon-streaked skyline of Tokyo, or sipping a perfectly pulled espresso in a bustling Buenos Aires café. You've done it. You've navigated the visa bureaucracy, packed your life into two oversized suitcases, and successfully relocated to another country. You are officially an expatriate, a digital nomad, a global citizen. You have left the United States behind.

Then, usually around late winter, a cold realization sets in. Or maybe it happens when a fellow American at a dinner party casually asks, "So, how are you handling your FBAR?"

You suddenly remember that while your body may have crossed an ocean, your financial identity is still tightly handcuffed to the Internal Revenue Service.

If you take a map of the world and highlight the countries that tax their citizens on their worldwide income regardless of where they actually live, you will end up coloring in exactly two places: the United States and Eritrea. That's it. If a Canadian moves to London, they stop paying Canadian taxes. If a German moves to Singapore, the German tax authorities wish them a fond farewell. But if you hold a navy blue passport with a bald eagle on the front—or a green card in your wallet—the IRS expects to hear from you every single year, until the day you die or legally renounce your status.

It does not matter if you haven't set foot on American soil in a decade. It doesn't matter if you earn your money in euros, yen, or pesos. It doesn't matter if your foreign employer has already withheld thirty percent of your paycheck for local taxes. As far as the US government is concerned, an American making a living in

Paris is fundamentally no different than an American making a living in Peoria.

This citizenship-based taxation system catches millions of expats off guard, turning an exciting international adventure into a source of low-grade, chronic anxiety. The rules are labyrinthine. The penalties for getting them wrong are notoriously draconian. And the conventional wisdom you find on internet forums is often a toxic cocktail of outdated loopholes, half-truths, and outright illegal advice.

But here is the truth that often gets lost in the panic: Living abroad does not mean you are destined to be double-taxed into oblivion. In fact, if you understand the levers, pulleys, and escape hatches built into the US tax code, you can legally and systematically reduce your US tax bill—often all the way to zero.

The purpose of the pages ahead is to strip away the dread and give you a clear, actionable mental model of the US expat tax landscape. You are not going to read a dry recitation of tax law. You are going to learn how to play defense, how to play offense, and how to build a bulletproof financial strategy that lets you actually enjoy your life overseas.

To do that, we have to fundamentally rewire how you think about your money.

The biggest conceptual hurdle for most new expats is realizing that international taxation is a two-front war. There is the tax you *pay*, and there is the information you *report*.

Most Americans assume that if they don't owe the IRS any money, they don't need to file anything. This is a perfectly logical assumption, and in the realm of international tax, it is completely wrong. The US government is profoundly suspicious of money that sits outside its borders. To monitor that money, Congress has enacted a sweeping ecosystem of disclosure forms.

You might owe zero dollars in actual income tax because you don't earn enough, or because you pay higher taxes in your host country. But if you have a local checking account in London to pay your rent, and you forget to file a piece of paper called the FBAR (Report of Foreign Bank and Financial Accounts) to tell the US Treasury about it, the penalty isn't a slap on the wrist. The penalty can be $10,000 per violation, per year. For an account that owes no tax. For an accidental omission.

This disconnect between tax liability and reporting penalties is what transforms ordinary teachers, freelance designers, and corporate managers into accidental outlaws. We are going to fix that. You will learn to recognize the reporting landmines before you step on them, mastering the alphabet soup of FBARs, FATCA, and Form 8938s, and discovering exactly which foreign accounts require a spotlight and which can remain comfortably private.

Once the reporting defenses are in place, the real strategy begins: minimizing the actual tax.

The US tax code provides heavy shields to protect expats from paying taxes twice on the same dollar, but these shields do not activate automatically. You have to choose them, and choosing the wrong one can cost you thousands of dollars and restrict your options for years to come.

You will master the Foreign Earned Income Exclusion (FEIE), a powerful provision that allows you to simply erase over a hundred thousand dollars of earned income from your US tax return. We will look at exactly how to qualify, whether through the strict day-counting of the Physical Presence Test or the more nuanced facts-and-circumstances approach of the Bona Fide Residence Test. You'll understand why your "tax home" matters more than your physical home, and how housing allowances can further stretch your tax-free limits.

But the FEIE is not a magic wand, and it's not always the smartest play. If you live in a high-tax country like Germany, Australia, or

Japan, invoking the FEIE might actually be a financial mistake. Instead, you'll learn to wield the Foreign Tax Credit (FTC)—a dollar-for-dollar offset against your US tax bill for the taxes you pay to your host country. You will see how these credits are sorted into different "baskets," how they carry over from year to year, and how mismatched tax calendars between countries can be managed. By the time you finish, you will know exactly when to use the FEIE, when to use the FTC, and how to confidently decide between the two without accidentally double-dipping.

Yet, taxes are not just about the paycheck you earn today; they are about the wealth you build for tomorrow. And this is where the borders truly start to blur.

What happens to your US retirement accounts when you move to a country that doesn't recognize a Roth IRA? What happens when you try to open a standard brokerage account in Europe, only to find that foreign mutual funds are classified by the IRS as Passive Foreign Investment Companies (PFICs)—a designation so punitively taxed and hopelessly complex that it can wipe out your entire investment return? You will learn how to navigate these investment pitfalls, classifying your passive income, dividends, and gains so you don't inadvertently trigger disastrous tax rates just by trying to save for the future.

We also have to deal with the lingering ghosts of your American past. Leaving the United States is one thing; breaking up with your specific home state is entirely another. Certain states—like California, New York, and Virginia—are notoriously reluctant to let their taxpayers go. You will learn the difference between residency and domicile, and discover why keeping a driver's license, voting in local elections, or maintaining a storage unit can inadvertently keep you hooked to a state income tax system long after you've moved to a different continent.

For the entrepreneurs, freelancers, and digital nomads, the complexity ratchets up another notch. If you are self-employed abroad, you might find yourself caught in a tug-of-war between the US Social Security system and your host country's equivalent. We will dissect the Totalization Agreements that prevent you from paying double payroll taxes, and break down the unexpected compliance nightmares that happen when you decide to incorporate a small business overseas. You'll learn why setting up a foreign corporation to run your freelance graphic design business might sound like a savvy offshore strategy, but could instead trigger a cascade of US reporting requirements that cost more in accounting fees than the business actually makes.

Ultimately, everything you are about to learn is geared toward one singular goal: execution. Technical knowledge is useless if you don't know how to apply it on a Tuesday afternoon when you are staring at a stack of foreign pay stubs, trying to figure out the right exchange rate to use on a Form 1040.

You will learn how to build a repeatable, low-stress filing workflow. You will know exactly what documentation you need to survive an audit, how to cleanly translate foreign currencies for the IRS, and how to logically organize your financial life so tax season becomes a minor administrative chore rather than a month-long panic attack. And if you are reading this right now with a sinking feeling in your stomach because you have lived abroad for three years and haven't filed a single US tax return—breathe. You are going to learn how to fix past noncompliance safely, responsibly, and legally through amnesty programs designed specifically for expats who honestly didn't know the rules.

Living abroad is one of the most intellectually rewarding, deeply transformative experiences a person can have. You are adapting to new cultures, learning new languages, and redefining what your life can look like. Your taxes should not be the anchor that drags you down.

The US tax system is a massive, intimidating machine. But it operates on logic, rules, and math. Once you understand the mechanics of the machine, you stop fearing it. You stop guessing. You start making confident, strategic decisions that keep more of your hard-earned money in your own pocket, no matter which hemisphere you happen to be standing in.

So, pour yourself another espresso, get comfortable, and let's get started.

Chapter 1

Understanding the US Expat Tax Landscape

Moving abroad can change your language, your landlord, and your lunch habits—but it usually does not erase your US tax life. This chapter helps readers replace vague anxiety with a clear map: who still has to file, why the rules exist, where the main tax breaks fit, and how to stay ahead of deadlines before small misunderstandings become expensive problems.

1.1 Who Counts as a US Taxpayer Abroad

The quickest way to get into trouble with US expat taxes is to confuse *distance* with *disconnection*. Living in Barcelona, Bangkok, or Buenos Aires can feel like you've stepped out of the American system—new language, new employer, new currency, maybe even a new passport. But the IRS doesn't measure your tax life in miles. It measures it in status. And a surprising number of people keep US filing and reporting obligations for years (sometimes decades) after their last US zip code.

A useful mindset: before asking, "Do I owe US tax?" ask, "Am I still a US taxpayer?" Those are different questions. Owing tax is about math. Being a US taxpayer is about whether the US considers you inside its tax net in the first place—and that can be true even when the math later works out to zero.

The two big categories: citizens and "resident aliens"

Most people abroad who still have a US tax relationship fall into one of two buckets.

US citizens are the obvious one. If you're a US citizen, the starting assumption is that you're a US taxpayer, regardless of where you live, what passport you use to board planes, or whether your paycheck comes from a foreign employer into a foreign bank.

The second bucket is less intuitive: *resident aliens*. That phrase doesn't mean "someone who lives in America right now." It's a technical tax term for certain non-citizens whom the US treats much like citizens for income tax purposes. If you've ever held a green card—or you spend enough time in the US in a way that trips the IRS's residency rules—you can fall into this category even if your everyday life is firmly planted abroad.

This is where many long-term expats get surprised. They left the US years ago, their work is overseas, their kids' schools are overseas, their bank accounts are overseas—and yet, their status can still point back to the United States.

US citizens abroad: the simplest rule, the widest reach

For a US citizen, the question usually isn't "Am I a US taxpayer?" It's "What do I have to file, and what do I have to disclose?"

A US return can be required even when:

- your income is earned entirely outside the US,
- you already paid tax to another country,
- you don't expect to owe the IRS anything after credits or exclusions,
- you haven't set foot in the US all year.

That last point is emotionally important. Many people assume physical presence is the decider. It isn't. Physical presence becomes relevant later, when you're trying to qualify for certain benefits or sort out technical definitions. But for basic filing identity—"Does the US consider me a taxpayer?"—citizenship alone is often enough.

There are edge cases, of course. Some people become US citizens as children and barely remember the paperwork. Some were born in the US while their parents were studying or working there and left as infants. Some have never applied for a US passport. Some consider themselves citizens "on paper" but not in practice. The IRS tends to care far more about what your legal status *is* than how central it feels to your identity.

If you are a US citizen abroad and you've been ignoring US filings because "I don't live there," the most helpful shift is to separate *filing* from *paying*. Filing is often the price of admission to the relief provisions that keep you from being taxed twice. Not filing can turn what would have been an administrative chore into a compliance cleanup.

Green card holders abroad: the status that follows you

Green card holders often assume that leaving the US ends their US tax life. Sometimes it does—but not automatically, and not just because your plane took off.

From a US tax perspective, holding a green card generally means the US treats you as a resident for income tax purposes under what's commonly called the *green card test*. That treatment can apply even if your actual home, job, and family life have moved overseas. In plain language: a green card is not just an immigration document; it can be a tax identity.

That creates a real-world trap. Many green card holders spend years abroad without thinking about US taxes because:

- their employer is foreign,

- their salary is paid in local currency,
- their social circle has moved on,
- they assume residency is about where you sleep at night.

But the IRS can still see a green card as a sign you're in the US tax net until you take steps to end that status. Immigration and tax don't always move in lockstep, and "I haven't used it" is not the same thing as "I don't have it."

There's also a more subtle version of this: someone who *thinks* they no longer have a green card because it expired, or because they stopped renewing it, or because they've been out of the US too long. An expired card is like an expired driver's license—it may not be useful for certain purposes, but it doesn't necessarily mean the underlying status evaporated. This is a place where assumptions can be expensive.

Non-citizens without green cards: the time-in-the-US factor

Even without citizenship or a green card, a person can become a US taxpayer under the *substantial presence test*. That's the IRS's way of saying, "If you spend enough time in the United States, we're going to treat you as a resident for tax purposes."

For many expats, this matters in the opposite direction: you live abroad but travel back to the US regularly—long summers, extended business trips, caring for family, remote work that happens to be performed in the US for stretches. Over time, the calendar can quietly build a case that you're a US tax resident for a particular year.

The key practical takeaway isn't to memorize a formula on first reading. It's to realize the IRS can treat residency like a math problem. If you're not a citizen and don't have a green card, your US taxpayer status can still flip on in a year where your US days add up, and flip off in a year where they don't. People who float between countries—consultants, airline crew, digital nomads, cross-border couples—often need to track days the way travelers track passport expiry dates: boring, but protective.

The treaty curveball (especially for green card holders)

Tax treaties can complicate the picture in an unintuitive way: a treaty might allow someone who otherwise looks like a US tax resident to be treated as a resident of another country under "tie-breaker" rules. That can matter for green card holders and others caught between definitions.

Here's the caution: treaties are not a magic cloaking device. Taking a treaty position can have ripple effects. It can change what forms you file, what you disclose, and how the IRS views your status for certain purposes. It's also fact-dependent—meaning the answer can change based on where your permanent home is, where your "center of vital interests" sits, and similar concepts that don't fit neatly into a spreadsheet.

Treaties are powerful tools, but they're also the kind of tool you handle with the instruction manual open. If you find yourself thinking, "A treaty probably means I don't have to file," treat that as a signal to slow down, not a conclusion.

"US person": the phrase that shows up on bank forms for a reason

Even if you don't think of yourself as a "taxpayer," foreign banks and brokers may force the question through their onboarding paperwork. Thanks to FATCA-driven compliance, institutions outside the US often ask whether you are a "US person."

That term is broader than "US resident." It can include US citizens, green card holders, and other categories depending on the specific rule being applied. Practically, when a bank asks, they're usually trying to determine whether they have US-related reporting responsibilities—and whether they should request a Form W-9 (for US persons) or a Form W-8BEN (for non-US persons).

This is why expats often discover their US status in the most mundane way possible: not through an IRS letter, but through a bank clerk calmly sliding a form across the desk. If a financial institution treats you as US-linked, it's worth taking that seriously. Their incentive is to reduce their own compliance risk, not to interpret the rules in the most generous way for you.

The filing trigger most people miss: you can have obligations even with "no tax due"

A lot of expats are surprised by how many US obligations are not really about paying tax. They're about reporting.

Two examples illustrate the point:

Income tax filing can be required even when foreign tax wipes out US tax. If your income is high enough to require a return based on normal filing thresholds, you may need to file Form 1040 even if exclusions or credits later reduce your US tax to zero. The return is still the container the IRS expects.

Financial account reporting can be required even when your income is modest. Many expats have ordinary local bank accounts—checking for rent, savings for emergencies, maybe an investment account because local employers or pension systems nudge you into one. Some US reporting rules are triggered by account balances, not by income. This is why someone can be fully taxed abroad, owe nothing to the US, and still have serious US compliance duties.

The emotional snag is that "no tax due" feels like it should mean "no problem." But the IRS runs on forms. If the rule says "file," the absence of tax is not a hall pass; it's just a common outcome after you file correctly.

A practical way to self-identify: the five-question reality check

Rather than trying to memorize every definition, use a short diagnostic that matches how expat life actually works. Answer these in order:

1. *Are you a US citizen?* If yes, assume you remain a US taxpayer unless you have taken formal steps to change that legal status.
2. *Do you have (or have you had) a green card?* If yes, don't assume the tax relationship ended just because you moved. The timing and manner of ending that status can matter.
3. *Did you spend significant time in the US this year or last?* If you're not a citizen and don't have a green card, days in the US can still create US tax residency for a given year.
4. *Did a foreign bank or broker classify you as a "US person" and request US tax forms?* Treat that as a clue that your status is US-linked, even if your life feels fully abroad.
5. *Do you have foreign financial accounts that ever held meaningful balances during the year?* Even if you're not sure about income tax filing, account reporting can create separate obligations.

If your answers make you pause, that's useful information. Uncertainty itself is a risk factor in expat taxes. People who are crystal-clear about their status tend to have simpler compliance. People who are vaguely unsure tend to accumulate years of "I'll deal with it later," which rarely makes anything easier.

Common expat profiles—and the misunderstanding that trips each one

Certain patterns repeat so often they're almost predictable.

The "I left at 22 and never looked back" US citizen. They built a life abroad and stopped thinking about the US. Often they're fully compliant locally and assume that's the whole story. Their blind spot is that the IRS doesn't measure loyalty; it measures citizenship and filing thresholds.

The green card holder who moved abroad "temporarily" and stayed. They kept the card "just in case" and didn't file because they weren't earning US income. The blind spot is that the green card can keep them in the US tax net even when the US plays no role in their cash flow.

The dual citizen who identifies as non-American. They may not use a US passport and may have little cultural connection to the US. The blind spot is that identity and obligation are not the same category in tax law.

The frequent flyer who lives abroad but spends long stretches in the US. They think "I'm not moving back" settles the question. The blind spot is that residency can be triggered by days, not intentions.

The accidental investor. They opened a local investment account because it's normal where they live—maybe even required for retirement savings—without realizing the US has its own taxonomy of foreign accounts and foreign entities. Their blind spot is that normal financial adulthood abroad can create US reporting complexity, even when the amounts are not extravagant.

None of these people are doing anything shady. They're doing normal life. The problem is that "normal life abroad" doesn't map neatly onto "normal paperwork" in the US system.

What it means to "exit" the US tax net (and why it's not the same as moving)

For US citizens, the legal act that changes taxpayer identity is generally not packing your bags; it's changing citizenship status. That's a serious decision with legal and personal consequences well beyond taxes, and it's not something people stumble into by accident.

For green card holders, the concept is different. Many assume that long absence automatically ends the status, but immigration status and tax status have their own rules and timelines. The cleanest approach is to treat this as a documentation question: *What does your legal record say now?* If the answer is fuzzy, the IRS world is rarely forgiving of fuzziness.

This is less about pushing anyone toward a specific choice and more about respecting reality: leaving the US physically is easy. Leaving the US tax system legally, if that's your goal, is a separate project.

The "I don't owe anything" trap: why filing can still be strategically valuable

Even if you suspect your US tax will be reduced to zero, filing can matter for reasons that feel almost unfairly practical:

- *Paper trails.* A filed return is a timestamped record of what you reported and when.
- *Access to elections and benefits.* Certain expat tax benefits and positions are claimed on a return; if you don't file, you don't claim.
- *Avoiding penalty landmines.* Some of the harshest expat penalties relate to missing information reporting, not unpaid income tax.

Think of a US return less like a bill and more like a standardized "annual report" about your tax life. Sometimes that annual report ends with a check to the IRS. Often, for expats, it ends with a zero. Either way, the IRS still expects the report when the rules say you're the kind of person who must provide one.

A final gut-check: if any of these phrases sound like you, pause before you assume you're done

Certain statements are common right before an expat discovers they had obligations they didn't know about:

- "I haven't lived in the US in years."
- "My employer is foreign, so it's not US income."
- "I pay plenty of tax where I live, so the US can't tax me too."
- "My green card expired, so I'm not a US person anymore."
- "It's just a local checking account."

Each sentence contains a reasonable human intuition. None of them, by themselves, determines whether you're in the US tax net.

The cleanest takeaway is also the simplest: if you are a US citizen, start from "yes, I'm a US taxpayer." If you hold or held a green card, treat your status as something to confirm rather than assume. If you're neither but spend meaningful time in the US, track days like they matter—because they can. And if a foreign bank treats you as US-linked, take the hint early, while the fix is still easy.

1.2 Why Living Abroad Does Not End Your US Tax Return

A lot of countries treat taxes like a cover charge: you pay because you're inside. Move out, and the bouncer stops asking for your ticket. The US tends to treat taxes more like a membership plan tied to who you *are* (and, for many long-term residents, what the US considers you to be), not simply where you happen to live on a Tuesday in March. That's why someone can have a life that's 100% foreign—foreign employer, foreign mortgage, foreign retirement plan, foreign school drop-off line—and still have a US Form 1040 in their future.

The practical result is less dramatic than it sounds. For many expats, the US return becomes an annual act of translation: converting a foreign financial life into US categories, then applying the set of rules designed to keep the same income from getting taxed twice. The surprise isn't that the US wants the paperwork. The surprise is how often the paperwork exists even when the check to the IRS doesn't.

"Worldwide income: the US cares about *what* you earned, not *where* the money was sitting"

"Worldwide income" can sound philosophical, like the IRS is trying to tax your entire existence. In reality, it's very literal: the US generally wants US taxpayers to report income from all sources—salary, freelance work, interest, dividends, capital gains—whether the payer is in Seattle or Singapore.

That includes income that doesn't *feel* like it has anything to do with the US. A few common examples:

- Your salary from a foreign employer deposited into a local bank account.
- Consulting income paid by non-US clients.
- Interest from a savings account at a foreign bank.
- Dividends from a foreign brokerage account.
- Rental income from an apartment you own in the country where you live.

The emotional mismatch is the hardest part. People associate taxation with roads, schools, and services—things that are obviously local. If your daily life is being powered by another country's infrastructure, it's natural to assume that country's tax return is the only one that matters. The US approach is different: you can be paying full freight where you live and still need to *tell* the US what happened financially over the year.

"I don't have US income" is usually a misunderstanding, not a fact

Expats often use "US income" to mean "income that came from the US." The IRS uses a different concept: if you're a US taxpayer, income is generally reportable on your US return even when it's foreign in every normal-person sense.

That misunderstanding is surprisingly sticky because it sounds reasonable in conversation. If your employer is a local school in France, how could that be "US income"? It isn't. But it can still be *US-reportable income.*

This difference matters because it changes the kind of planning you do. If you assume "no US income" means "no US return," you don't plan—you drift. If you understand that foreign wages and foreign investments can still land on a US tax return, you start asking better questions early: How will the US treat my pension contributions? Are my foreign taxes high enough to offset US tax? Do I need extra reporting for accounts?

Why double taxation happens (and why it often doesn't end up as a true double bill)

Once you accept that the US wants the same global income story you're already telling your current country, the next fear shows up fast: "So I'll pay tax twice?"

Double taxation is a real possibility. Here's the simplest way it happens:

1. You live and work in a foreign country. That country taxes your wages because you live there, work there, or both.
2. The US also expects a return that includes those wages because you're still a US taxpayer.

On paper, that looks like two tax collectors reaching for the same paycheck. In practice, a full double hit is often softened—

or eliminated—by a set of relief rules. The US system essentially admits the problem and then offers mechanisms that reduce or reshape the US tax result.

The catch is that these mechanisms don't behave like interchangeable coupons. They have different sweet spots, different limits, and different side effects. Choosing the right tool (or combination) can be the difference between "annoying paperwork" and "unexpected tax."

It also helps to think about *timing*. Many countries tax income in ways that don't line up neatly with the US calendar year, and taxes might be paid later than the year the income is earned. The US still wants a yearly report. That mismatch can create confusion even when the long-term outcome is fair.

The three main relief valves: exclude, credit, or recharacterize

When expats talk about "not paying US tax," they're usually talking about one of three mechanisms:

- *The Foreign Earned Income Exclusion* (*FEIE*) (claimed on Form 2555), which can allow qualifying expats to exclude a portion of foreign *earned* income from US taxation.
- *The Foreign Tax Credit* (*FTC*) (often computed on Form 1116), which can reduce US tax by crediting certain foreign taxes you paid or accrued.
- *Treaty-based benefits*, which can change how particular types of income are taxed (or which country gets first claim) under an income tax treaty.

All three exist for the same reason—so the US system doesn't routinely produce absurd results for people living normal lives abroad—but they solve the problem in different ways.

One way to keep them straight: FEIE is about *removing* certain earned income from the US tax base, the FTC is about *offsetting*

US tax with foreign tax, and treaties are often about *relabeling or assigning* taxing rights for specific categories of income.

And yes, it's possible to feel like you "should" qualify for all of them at once. The rules don't always let you stack benefits freely. A lot of expat tax mistakes come from treating these provisions like three separate gifts rather than three parts of one system.

A quick reality check using three expats

Concrete scenarios make the logic click faster than abstract rules.

Software engineer in a higher-tax country. She pays a high local income tax rate and has no US employer. The US still asks for her worldwide income, but foreign tax credits often wipe out most or all US tax on that same income. Her US return becomes proof that the income existed and that the foreign tax was paid—less a bill, more a reconciliation.

Teacher abroad early in the year. He moved overseas in February and is excited to hear about the FEIE. But some benefits depend on meeting timing tests. He may still be a US taxpayer the entire year while he waits for the calendar to cooperate. That means filing decisions can become timing decisions—especially in the first year abroad.

"No US income" freelancer with local bank accounts. She invoices clients in local currency and keeps the money in a local bank. She might owe little or nothing to the IRS after applying the right relief, but she can still have US filing and separate reporting obligations. The absence of US *tax due* doesn't automatically mean the absence of US *paperwork*.

These aren't exotic people with offshore empires. They're the default expat cast. The surprise is how normal lives create US reporting footprints.

When the US return feels like a second opinion, not a second tax

A useful reframing: the US return often functions like a second opinion on your financial year. Your country of residence makes the first diagnosis—how much tax you owe locally, how retirement contributions are treated, what deductions exist. The US then asks you to restate the same facts in US terms and calculates what *would* be due under US rules, *then* applies exclusions, credits, and treaty positions where appropriate.

This can feel redundant, because it is. It can also feel invasive, because it sometimes is—especially when foreign account reporting enters the picture. But the logic is consistent: worldwide income comes in, US tax is computed under US rules, then relief provisions prevent or reduce double taxation.

Where expats get burned is not the basic logic; it's the assumption that "I'm taxed elsewhere" automatically closes the loop. It often closes the tax loop. It does not always close the filing and reporting loop.

The fine print that matters in real life: not all income is "earned," and not all taxes are creditable

"Foreign income" is not a single bucket. The US divides your financial life into categories, and the relief tools apply differently across them.

FEIE generally targets *earned income*—compensation for work. It doesn't typically shelter your dividends, capital gains, interest, or rental income. That's why some expats with modest salaries but significant investment income can still face US tax even if their wages are largely neutralized.

The foreign tax credit is broader in spirit—it's designed to prevent the same income from being taxed twice—but it still has limitations. Credits are calculated under rules that can restrict how much foreign tax you can use in a given year and how categories of income interact. That's how someone can honestly say, "I paid a lot of foreign tax," and still have a US tax bill in a particular year due to category limits or timing mismatches.

Treaties can be elegant in narrow situations and irrelevant in others. A treaty might provide a favorable rule for a pension distribution, a specific type of employment income, or certain investment income. But a treaty is not a blanket permission slip. It's more like a set of very specific traffic signals on a complicated intersection: helpful when you're at that intersection, useless when you're not.

Why "just don't file" is the most expensive strategy that feels cheap

There's a particular kind of expat logic that shows up when life is already complicated: "If I'm not going to owe anything, why invite the hassle?" It's a tempting thought—especially if you've had years where your local tax return was already a full-contact sport.

The problem is that the US system often makes filing the gateway to being treated fairly. The relief tools that prevent double taxation generally don't apply automatically to people who simply disappear. If you don't file, you're not declining a bill; you're declining to submit the evidence and elections that produce the zero bill in the first place.

There's also a psychological trap: once you skip one year, the second year feels harder, because now you're "behind." Skipping becomes a habit disguised as a choice. Then a bank asks about US status, or a job requires US compliance, or you decide you want to move back for family reasons—and suddenly "I don't owe anything" turns into a paperwork recovery project.

Why the US insists on the return even when the end result is zero

From the taxpayer's point of view, a zero balance feels like the only number that should matter. From the IRS's point of view, the return is how the system:

- determines whether you *would* owe US tax under US rules,
- verifies whether you qualify for the relief you're claiming,
- tracks categories of income that may be treated differently,
- supports information reporting regimes that sit alongside the tax calculation.

That last point—information reporting—is where many expats feel blindsided. The US has separate reporting systems for foreign accounts and assets, and government reviewers have documented how overlapping rules create friction and confusion for taxpayers abroad. Even when the income tax result is simple, the reporting layer can be where the work hides.

None of this makes the process emotionally satisfying. It does make it predictable. If you start from the premise that the US wants a full yearly picture, the rest of the system—relief provisions included—makes more sense.

The simplest takeaway that stays true in messy lives

Living abroad doesn't end your US tax return because the US starts from worldwide income for US taxpayers, then uses exclusions, credits, and treaty rules to keep that policy from producing routine double taxation. The return is where all of that gets reconciled.

That's why the right question is rarely "Do I owe the IRS money?" The better question is "Which set of rules will I use to get from worldwide income to a fair US result—and what do I need to file to claim that result?"

1.3 How a US Return Works for Expats

Most expat tax anxiety comes from a simple illusion: that there's a special "expat tax return" with its own rules, its own math, and its own mysterious trapdoors. In real life, the IRS doesn't run two different income tax systems. Expats generally file the same Form 1040 as everyone else. The expat-specific rules show up as attachments—extra forms that change what gets taxed, when it gets taxed, or what gets disclosed.

That's good news, because Form 1040 is less like a maze and more like a story with a predictable plot. Money shows up. Some of it gets carved away by adjustments and deductions. A tax is calculated on what remains. Credits reduce that tax. Payments are compared to the final number. Then you either owe or you don't. Expat rules don't replace that story—they lean on it.

The return as a narrative: from "what happened" to "what's owed"

A US tax return is basically the IRS asking: "Tell me what happened financially, in categories I understand." The categories matter. The IRS doesn't want your life as a diary entry. It wants your life as sortable data.

At a high level, think of the return in four phases:

1. *Report income.* This is where worldwide income shows up—wages, self-employment income, interest, dividends, capital gains, rental income, and more.
2. *Reduce income.* Certain "above—the-line" adjustments can reduce the income that gets taxed.
3. *Calculate tax.* Apply progressive tax rates (the bracket system) to taxable income.

4. *Reduce the tax.* Credits can reduce the tax bill dollar-for-dollar, then payments/withholding determine the final balance due or refund.

If you keep that sequence in your head, expat provisions become easier to place. The Foreign Earned Income Exclusion affects the income side. The Foreign Tax Credit affects the tax side. Treaty positions can affect categorization. Information reporting lives alongside all of it, sometimes on the return, sometimes completely outside it.

Step one: income goes on the return even if you plan to "remove" it later

Here's a counterintuitive truth that saves a lot of confusion: you often start by reporting the full income even when you know you'll later exclude it or offset the tax with credits.

That can feel backwards. If your salary is earned in another country and you qualify for relief, why put it on a US return at all? Because the IRS wants to see the starting point. Many expat benefits work as modifications to the calculation, not a free pass to omit the underlying facts.

So your foreign wages generally still appear as wages on Form 1040. Your foreign freelance income still appears as self-employment income. Your foreign dividends still look like dividends. The return is built to accept global inputs; the relief provisions are how you prevent those inputs from being taxed twice.

This is also why "I already paid tax abroad" doesn't change the first move. Paying foreign tax is usually relevant later, when you calculate the Foreign Tax Credit. The return still begins with: what did you earn?

Earned income vs. "money that just shows up": why categories matter more abroad

In ordinary conversation, income is income. On a US return, income is a set of different species, and expats feel that taxonomy more sharply because a lot of foreign financial life doesn't fit US instincts.

The biggest divide is between *earned income* (money you get from working) and *unearned income* (money you get from owning things—investments, property, certain distributions). This split matters because some expat tools target earned income more directly than investment income.

A few everyday expat examples:

- Your paycheck from a foreign employer: earned income.
- Your income from freelancing/contracting: earned income.
- Dividends from a foreign brokerage account: investment income.
- Interest from a local savings account: investment income.
- Rental income from your apartment abroad: rental income (its own rules).
- Capital gains from selling shares or property: capital gains (often taxed differently than wages).

Once you see these as separate lanes, the logic of expat planning becomes clearer: you're not choosing one magic tool for "foreign income." You're deciding how each lane will be treated on your US return.

Step two: adjustments and deductions—the "diet" part of the return

After income is reported, the return asks: "What parts of this should be reduced before we apply tax rates?" This is where deductions and certain adjustments matter.

Most expats take the *standard deduction* rather than itemizing, just like most taxpayers in the US. The standard deduction is the IRS saying, "We'll assume some baseline deductible amount, no receipts required." Itemized deductions can still matter for some expats—especially those with unusual situations—but for many, itemizing is like carrying around a bag of coins to avoid tapping your credit card: technically possible, often not worth it.

What's easy to miss is that expat provisions can interact with deductions. If you exclude some income, that can affect how certain deductions or credits are calculated or limited. Even when a return ends at zero, the internal mechanics still matter, because the IRS wants the math to be coherent.

The moment everyone forgets: filing status is still a big deal abroad

Living abroad doesn't make filing status irrelevant. In fact, expat life can make filing status more complicated.

Filing status—single, married filing jointly, married filing separately, head of household—affects tax brackets, deductions, and eligibility for certain benefits. Two people with the same combined income can have different US outcomes depending on how they file.

Some expats assume "married filing jointly" is always best because it feels like the default. Sometimes it is. Sometimes it isn't—especially when one spouse is not a US taxpayer, or when foreign financial accounts and reporting become part of the equation.

Filing status is also where expat life gets emotionally real. A marriage can be perfectly healthy while being administratively messy: different citizenships, different countries of residence, different bank accounts, different retirement plans, different tolerance for paperwork. The US return demands a clean category anyway. The best filing status is often the one that produces the lowest overall cost *and* the least risk, not necessarily the one that feels most "normal."

Step three: tax rates and brackets still apply—even when special expat rules exist

The US uses progressive tax rates: the more taxable income you have, the higher the marginal rate on the top portion. That's familiar. What's less familiar is how expat provisions can change the *shape* of the income that ends up being taxed.

A common misconception is that expat benefits "turn off" US tax brackets. They don't. They change what lands inside the bracket system.

This is why two expats with identical salaries can have different US outcomes:

- One lives in a country with high income taxes and uses foreign tax credits to offset US tax.
- Another lives in a country with low income taxes and relies more heavily on excluding earned income.

Even if both end up owing little or nothing, the path to that result is different. And the path matters because it can affect other pieces of the return: how investment income is taxed, whether certain credits apply, and what documentation is needed.

Where expat tools plug in: Form 2555 and Form 1116 as "attachments," not alternate universes

The core architecture stays Form 1040. The expat magic happens in the attachments.

Form 2555 is the usual attachment for claiming the Foreign Earned Income Exclusion (and, if applicable, foreign housing benefits). It's eligibility-driven: it asks you to demonstrate that you qualify, and then it calculates the amount you can exclude.

Form 1116 is commonly used to compute the Foreign Tax Credit. It's the form that turns "I paid foreign tax" into "here's the credit allowed on my US return," under the IRS limitations and categories. Some simplified situations can allow a credit without Form 1116, but many expats end up in Form 1116 territory quickly—especially if they have multiple types of income or foreign taxes that don't map neatly to a single bucket.

A helpful mental model: Form 2555 changes the *income side* of the story; Form 1116 changes the *tax side* of the story. You can't really understand either one in isolation, because both are designed to feed numbers back into the Form 1040 calculation.

A practical decision point: exclude income or credit foreign tax?

Many expats are forced into an early choice: do you try to remove some foreign earned income from US taxation, or do you keep it taxable but use foreign tax credits to offset the US tax?

This isn't a moral choice; it's engineering. You're trying to build the most stable structure with the fewest unwanted side effects.

Some realities that shape the decision:

- If you live in a higher-tax country, foreign tax credits often do a lot of heavy lifting. You may end up with little US tax due because the foreign tax already paid is substantial.

- If you live in a lower-tax country, excluding earned income can be more valuable because foreign tax credits may not be large enough to offset US tax on wages.
- If you have meaningful investment income, excluding earned income may not address the part of your financial life that still creates US tax.
- Timing matters in the first year abroad: eligibility for certain benefits depends on meeting specific tests, and you may not have met them by the time you're trying to file.

The key is not to assume one tool is always "the expat tool." Both are common. Both can lead to low or zero US tax. They just get there differently.

Credits: the part of the return that can make a bill disappear

Once the return calculates a preliminary tax, credits can reduce it. A *credit* is powerful because it reduces tax dollar-for-dollar. A $1,000 credit reduces your tax by $1,000. That's different from a deduction, which merely reduces the income you're taxed on.

The Foreign Tax Credit lives in this part of the story. It's one of the main ways the US avoids taxing the same foreign-source income twice. But it's not a blank check. The IRS doesn't let you use unlimited foreign tax credits against any kind of US tax. There are limitation calculations and income categories involved. This is where expat taxes stop being philosophically annoying and become computationally annoying.

Still, the big picture is reassuring: many expats reach a low or zero US tax result not because the IRS forgot about them, but because the credit mechanism does exactly what it's designed to do when the facts line up.

Payments and withholding: the final comparison that determines "refund or balance due"

After credits, the return asks: how much have you already paid toward this tax?

For many expats, US withholding is minimal or nonexistent because their employer is foreign. That doesn't automatically create a problem, but it changes the rhythm of your tax year. Instead of "withholding all year then reconcile," it may become "reconcile and then pay," or "make estimated payments if needed."

This is also where expats can feel whiplash. You can do everything right—report income, claim credits, compute a modest US tax—and still end up owing simply because nothing was withheld. The return isn't punishing you; it's just adding up the math.

The compliance stack: income tax is only part of what the US may want

A US expat filing season can be quiet on the income tax side and loud on the reporting side.

Two major reporting regimes often enter the picture:

- *Form 8938* (Statement of Specified Foreign Financial Assets), which is filed with your tax return when thresholds are exceeded. It's part of the FATCA regime.
- *FBAR* (FinCEN reporting for foreign financial accounts), which is *not* filed with your tax return. It's filed separately through FinCEN's system.

Those two bullets contain a lot of practical pain. The forms can cover similar territory—foreign bank accounts, for example—yet they are separate requirements administered under different authorities. Government reviewers have pointed to overlap and confusion here, and expats feel it directly: the same accounts can trigger multiple obligations, with different thresholds and different filing pathways.

There's another nuance that matters more than it should: Form 8938 sits inside your tax return, and its instructions discuss consequences for failing to file or report assets—including statute-of-limitations effects. In plain language, missing certain foreign asset reporting can keep your tax year "open" longer. That's not the kind of consequence people imagine when they think "I don't owe any tax."

So, when someone says, "My expat return is simple," it's worth asking: do they mean the tax calculation, or do they mean the full compliance package?

Why expat returns feel harder than domestic returns, even when the numbers are small

It's rarely the arithmetic that makes expat taxes exhausting. It's the translation layer:

- Foreign pay slips don't look like W-2s.
- Foreign tax years and payment schedules may not match the US calendar year.
- Local retirement accounts don't always map neatly onto US retirement categories.
- Foreign banks and brokers create account statements in unfamiliar formats and languages.

That's why even a modest-income expat with a normal job can feel overwhelmed. The work is gathering, converting, categorizing, and documenting—not inventing money, not hiding money, just making the year legible to a system built around US paperwork.

The comforting part is that the story stays the same each year. Once you understand where each piece plugs in—income first, adjustments and deductions, tax computation, credits, payments, then separate reporting obligations—the process becomes less mystical. It becomes a recurring administrative task with known pressure points.

A simple way to read your own return without becoming a tax professional

If you want to be able to sanity-check your own filings (or understand what a preparer is doing), focus on a few anchor questions:

- What are the major income categories being reported (wages, self-employment, interest/dividends, capital gains)?
- Is relief being applied by excluding income (Form 2555) or by crediting foreign taxes (often Form 1116), or both in a coordinated way?
- After deductions and adjustments, what taxable income remains, and what brackets are being applied?
- What credits are reducing the computed tax?
- What payments/withholding exist, and does that explain why there's a balance due or refund?
- Are there separate reporting obligations being satisfied (Form 8938 with the return; FBAR through FinCEN)?

You don't need to memorize every line of Form 1040 to be informed. But if you can follow the plot—income in, tax computed, tax reduced, payments compared—you'll catch the most common misunderstandings before they become expensive.

And that's the real goal: not to turn you into a tax preparer, but to make sure the US return stops feeling like a foreign language written in your native alphabet.

1.4 Deadlines, Extensions, and the Annual Compliance Calendar

Deadlines are where perfectly honest expats get turned into "noncompliant taxpayers" on paper. Not because they're hiding money, but because life abroad has a way of making April 15 feel like a rumor from a different planet. Your salary statement arrives late. Your local tax documents use a different year. Your accountant is on holiday when the US wants answers. Suddenly you're not "late on a form." You're late on an entire system that assumes you live a domestic, January-to-December, W-2-shaped life.

The fix is less heroic than people think. Compliance gets dramatically easier when it becomes a routine with recurring dates, not a yearly emergency where you improvise under stress. The goal isn't to worship deadlines. It's to use them the way you use flight times: fixed points that let you plan everything else.

The baseline due date still matters—even if you live elsewhere

For most individual taxpayers on a calendar year, the regular US filing deadline is April 15. Expats often hear that and shrug, because they've also heard "you get extra time." Both statements can be true at the same time, and that's where people get burned.

April 15 is the reference point the IRS uses to measure several things, including when interest starts running on unpaid tax. If you keep only one sentence in your head, make it this one: *more time to file is not automatically more time to pay.*

That distinction feels petty until it costs money. An extension can protect you from certain late-filing penalties. It does not magically freeze the calendar on what you owe.

The automatic expat extension: real, helpful, and widely misunderstood

Many taxpayers who are abroad on the regular due date qualify for an automatic two-month extension to file. In everyday life, this is the IRS acknowledging that international paperwork moves at international speed. The typical effect for calendar-year filers is that the filing deadline moves from April 15 to June 15.

There's a catch that feels almost too bureaucratic to be real: the IRS instructs taxpayers to attach a statement when they file explaining which qualifying situation applied. It's not a separate form request. It's more like a sticky note that says, "Here's why I'm allowed to use the automatic rule."

The automatic extension is a gift, but it's not a permission slip to ignore spring entirely. June 15 arrives quickly when you're waiting on documents from multiple countries, especially if you're converting currency, translating statements, or trying to reconcile taxes that were assessed on a different schedule.

The part that stings: interest can still start from the regular due date

Here's the detail that catches a lot of people on their first year abroad: even if you qualify for the automatic extension to file, interest may still accrue from the regular due date on any unpaid tax.

That means someone can do what feels like the *responsible* thing—file by June 15—and still pay interest because they didn't pay by April 15.

A simple example makes it concrete. Imagine you're self-employed in a place where clients pay slowly and no one withholds US tax for you. You file on June 10, well within your automatic expat extension window, and you pay your US balance that same day. If the balance should have been paid by

April 15, the IRS can still charge interest for the period between April 15 and June 10. It's not a moral judgment; it's just how the rules are written.

This is why experienced expats treat spring as two separate deadlines: a *payment* deadline and a *paperwork* deadline.

How to buy more time beyond June 15: Form 4868 (and the "pay to extend" trick)

If June 15 isn't enough, you can usually request additional time to file. The classic method is filing Form 4868, which is the standard US extension request for individuals. This is the tool that tends to push the filing deadline later in the year (often to October 15 for calendar-year filers).

IRS Topic No. 304 also notes another practical route: you can get an extension by making a payment designated as an extension, using IRS-approved payment methods. That's a useful trick for people who don't want to mail anything, don't want to wrestle with a form at the last minute, or simply want proof that they acted.

Two important boundaries around this idea:

- An extension is about filing paperwork, not about postponing your tax bill.
- Extensions are only as good as the estimate you base them on. If you underpay significantly, you can still face interest and potentially penalties.

Think of Form 4868 as buying time to finish the story, not buying time to avoid the ending.

Form 2350: the "I'm not eligible yet" extension that exists for a very specific reason

Some expats don't need more time because they're disorganized. They need more time because the calendar hasn't allowed them to qualify for FEIE-related benefits yet.

That's why Form 2350 exists. It's a special extension for taxpayers who expect to file Form 2555 and need additional time to meet the bona fide residence test or physical presence test for the Foreign Earned Income Exclusion (and related housing benefits). In plain language: you may know you're going to qualify, but you haven't been abroad long enough *yet* to satisfy the test by the time you'd otherwise need to file.

This is especially common in the first year abroad. Someone moves mid-year, starts a job overseas, and hears about the "330 full days" concept tied to the physical presence test. They look at the calendar and realize: by the time the return is due (even with the automatic two-month extension), they literally cannot have accumulated enough qualifying days yet.

Form 2350 is designed to avoid the awkward "file now, amend later" loop. It's a form with a purpose, not a general escape hatch. It must be filed by the due date that applies to you (often June 15 for qualifying expats, not April 15), which is another reason to keep your personal calendar straight.

Weekend and holiday drift: why "the deadline" can move without warning

One of the quieter sources of confusion is that due dates can shift when they fall on weekends or holidays. Most people only learn this after they've already made plans around the wrong day.

The practical move is not to obsess over the exact date each year. It's to build a routine that assumes deadlines can shift slightly and that you will confirm the exact date for the year you're filing. Treat mid-April, mid-June, and mid-October as your anchors, then verify the precise day once you're working in that filing season.

Your annual calendar needs two tracks: filing deadlines and reporting deadlines

A US expat's compliance year isn't just "the tax return." It's a set of overlapping obligations that don't always share the same filing path.

One of the biggest examples: FBAR. As noted earlier, FBAR is not filed with your tax return. It must be filed through FinCEN's e-filing system. That separation is the kind of detail that's easy to forget when you're focused on finishing Form 1040 and whatever attachments go with it.

This creates a common failure mode: someone files an extension for their Form 1040 and assumes everything else is automatically extended or "handled." But an extension for your income tax return does not automatically file your FBAR for you. FBAR lives in a different administrative universe.

The best way to prevent this is to treat reporting obligations as their own checklist item in your calendar, not as an afterthought stapled to the tax return.

Estimated taxes: the boring tool that keeps you from a nasty surprise

If you have a traditional US job, withholding does a lot of the work quietly. Many expats don't have that luxury. You might be self-employed, paid as a contractor, earning investment income, or working for an employer that doesn't withhold US tax. In those cases, *estimated taxes* can become your best friend.

Estimated payments are exactly what they sound like: you pay the IRS during the year based on what you expect to owe, rather than waiting for the return to tell you at the end. This helps in three ways:

- It smooths cash flow. A large April balance due can feel like a financial ambush.
- It can reduce interest and penalties tied to underpayment.
- It makes tax season psychologically lighter, because you're reconciling rather than scrambling.

You don't have to love estimated taxes. You just have to respect that the IRS calendar doesn't care whether your income arrives neatly or in bursts.

Building a repeatable routine: a practical expat compliance rhythm

A dependable calendar beats a heroic sprint every year. A simple rhythm many expats adopt looks like this:

- *January–February:* gather income documents, confirm local tax forms and timing, download annual statements from overseas accounts while they're easy to access.
- *March:* do a rough US estimate—especially if you might owe—so April doesn't become an unpleasant surprise.
- *April:* treat this as the "pay attention" month even if you won't file yet; if you expect to owe, consider paying by the regular due date to reduce interest.
- *May–June:* finalize and file if using the automatic abroad extension; attach the required statement explaining eligibility.
- *Summer–early fall:* if you extended further, use the time to resolve the hard parts rather than simply postponing; this is when people finally reconcile foreign taxes paid versus accrued, confirm exchange rates used, and double-check reporting thresholds.

The point isn't that your year must look like this. The point is that the work has a natural order. When you do the estimation early and the reconciliation later, deadlines stop feeling like traps and start feeling like appointments.

The best "extension strategy" is psychological: use extra time to reduce risk, not to postpone discomfort

Extensions are often treated like permission to procrastinate. The more effective way to treat them is as time to improve accuracy.

Extra time is valuable when you use it to:

- obtain missing documents from overseas institutions,
- confirm how local taxes map to US categories,
- sort out whether you're claiming relief through Form 2555 or Form 1116 (or both in a coordinated way),
- review foreign asset reporting obligations carefully rather than guessing.

Extra time is wasted when it's used to delay opening the folder labeled "Taxes."

The uncomfortable truth: filing late is rarely the biggest danger. Filing wrong—especially with international reporting—can be far more consequential. Time is most valuable when it makes the filing correct and complete.

A few rules that keep you out of last-minute chaos

Some habits are boring in the way smoke detectors are boring: you only notice them when they aren't there.

- Keep a running spreadsheet (or note) of overseas accounts, maximum balances, and where statements live. Don't trust yourself to reconstruct the year from memory.

- Save tax payment confirmations and extension confirmations like they're boarding passes. When something goes wrong, proof matters.
- If you're relying on qualifying tests for Form 2555 in your first year abroad, mark the date you expect to satisfy them. The calendar is part of your tax position.
- Treat the regular due date as a *payment checkpoint* even when you'll file later. If you might owe, paying earlier can reduce interest.

None of this is glamorous. That's the point. The expats who feel calm about compliance aren't smarter; they're more scheduled.

The payoff: when the calendar is predictable, everything else gets easier

Once the dates are on your calendar in a way you trust, expat taxes become less like a yearly crisis and more like maintaining a household across borders. You still have to do the work. But you're doing it on purpose, with time, and with a clear separation between what must be filed, what must be paid, and what must be reported somewhere else entirely.

That's how you avoid the most expensive expat tax mistake of all: assuming that because your life is international, the IRS deadline is optional.

Chapter 2

Residency, Tax Home, and Classifying Your Income

Most expat tax mistakes start with a simple misunderstanding: people try to claim a benefit before they have correctly labeled the income, the country, and the facts of their daily life. This chapter gives readers the sorting system behind the whole expat tax puzzle, so later decisions about FEIE, foreign tax credits, treaties, and state tax exposure feel less like guesswork and more like strategy.

2.1 Sorting Income into the Right Buckets

A lot of overseas tax confusion comes from a perfectly modern habit: treating your bank account like a blender. Salary drops in. A client pays an invoice. A dividend arrives. You sell a few shares. Rent hits the account. It all becomes "money I got this year," and it all feels interchangeable because it all spends the same.

The IRS does not share that view. The IRS treats your financial life less like a single stream and more like a set of pipes with different valves, pressure limits, and leak detectors. If you try to run everything through one pipe—especially the "I live abroad so it's probably excluded" pipe—you'll get surprises: a credit you can't claim, an exclusion that doesn't apply, or a self-employment wrinkle you didn't know existed until it shows up as a balance due.

The most useful early move isn't to hunt for loopholes. It's to label each dollar by *what it is*. Once the labels are right, the best tools tend to reveal themselves.

Bucket thinking: the IRS's version of "what kind of money is this?"

When people say "my income," they usually mean "my lifestyle." The IRS means "the legal character of each item." Two payments can be identical amounts deposited on the same day into the same account, yet be taxed under totally different rules because the IRS cares about the origin story.

For most Americans living outside the U.S., the income stories that matter most fall into four everyday buckets:

- *Compensation for work you do for someone else* (your paycheck life).
- *Compensation for work you do for yourself* (your invoice life).
- *Returns on money you already have* (your portfolio life).
- *Retirement and deferred compensation* (your "paid later" life).

Those aren't the only categories in the tax code, but they're the ones that decide whether an exclusion is even on the menu, which forms appear, and where many expats accidentally double-count (or fail to count) something.

Salary and wages: the cleanest bucket, until it isn't

A paycheck is the most straightforward kind of income to classify—right up until you receive it abroad and assume that geography turns it into something else. Pay from employment is generally "compensation for services." That label matters because many of the expat-friendly rules were built for this exact scenario: a person working outside the U.S. on a real job with real pay.

The trap is thinking that the word "salary" automatically means "qualifies for the Foreign Earned Income Exclusion." That exclusion is picky. It cares not only that you're paid for services, but also *where the services were performed* and the broader set of qualifying conditions that sit behind the scenes. So the first classification question is not "Did I earn it?" but "Is this pay for services, and can I trace those services to days and locations?"

A second trap is assuming the paycheck is the whole story. International employers love "total compensation" packages, and those packages can include items that are still treated as compensation even though they don't look like cash. Housing provided by an employer, meals, a car allowance, school fees, relocation benefits—sometimes these are taxable, sometimes partially excludable, sometimes handled under a local system in ways that don't map neatly to the U.S. return. The point is simpler than the details: if you're receiving value because you work there, the IRS may treat that value as pay. The bank deposit isn't the boundary; the employment relationship is.

A practical habit that saves pain later: keep a one-page "pay breakdown" for the year. Base salary, bonus, equity compensation, and every perk that has a number attached to it. If the employer reports it on a non-U.S. payslip in a way that doesn't resemble a W-2, you still want your own translation.

Bonuses, commissions, and "thank you" money: still the paycheck bucket

Bonuses and commissions feel like different species—unpredictable, seasonal, sometimes paid long after the work that generated them. For classification purposes, they usually belong in the same bucket as wages because they're still compensation for services.

Where expats get clipped is timing and geography. A bonus paid in March might be for a performance period that spanned multiple countries, or it might reward work done partly in the U.S. during a short business trip. If you lump the bonus into "foreign pay" because you happened to be living abroad when it hit your account, you can misclassify what portion ties to foreign work versus U.S. work. That mislabeling doesn't just affect what can be excluded; it can cascade into foreign tax credit math, sourcing, and withholding issues.

The fix is unglamorous but effective: treat variable compensation like a documentable story. What period did it cover? Where were you physically working during that period? If you can't answer those questions later, you're forced into rough estimates when you least want them.

Equity compensation: the bucket that looks like investing but behaves like pay

Stock-based compensation is where otherwise organized people lose the plot. Restricted stock units (RSUs), stock options, and similar awards create a powerful illusion: "I received stock, therefore this is investment income." Often, it's not. Frequently, it's still compensation—just delivered in a fancier container.

That matters because the "compensation" part and the "investment" part can both exist, but at different moments. There may be a compensation event when the award vests or when an option is exercised, and then there may be a capital gain or loss when the resulting shares are sold. If you treat the entire thing as a capital gain, you can misreport the compensation portion; if you treat the whole thing as wages, you can miss the later gain or loss.

For expats, equity pay is also a geography puzzle. Awards often relate to a work period that spans countries. You might have been granted options while in the U.S., moved abroad, and then had them vest while overseas. The "type of income" question (pay vs gain) comes first; only then does the "where is it sourced" question make sense.

A helpful mental model: stock compensation is often "pay first, investing second." It may *end* its life as a brokerage sale, but it often *begins* its life as compensation for labor.

Freelance and contract work: similar money, different rule set

Freelancing is a great example of why buckets matter. If you do the same work you used to do as an employee—say, design, consulting, software development—the money feels identical. The IRS treats it differently because the legal relationship is different.

Independent contractor income is typically business income. That can unlock deductions (legitimate business expenses can reduce the taxable profit), but it also drags in its own machinery: bookkeeping, profit-and-loss calculations, and potentially separate tax regimes and reporting requirements that don't apply to employees.

The most common expat mistake here is emotional, not mathematical: "I already pay plenty of tax overseas, so my U.S. return shouldn't be complicated." But complexity isn't a punishment; it's a classification consequence. When you're self-employed, the IRS wants to see the business as a business, not as a paycheck with extra steps.

Another common trap is mixing a "side gig" into your salary bucket because it's small. Small doesn't mean ignorable. A few thousand dollars of contract work might still change the form set you file, the way you track expenses, and how you coordinate exclusions or credits.

A clean practice: treat every freelance stream as if you might someday need to explain it to a skeptical stranger. Who paid you? What did you deliver? What expenses were necessary to do the work? What country were you in when you did it? If you can answer those questions, you've already done most of the hard part.

Reimbursements and allowances: not all "work-related" payments are equal

Expats are often paid through a patchwork: a base salary, then separate payments for housing, cost-of-living adjustments, education, travel, and "settling-in" costs. Some of these are true reimbursements under an accountable plan-like setup (meaning you incurred expenses and provided receipts), while others are simply allowances (meaning the employer gives you cash and you decide what to do with it).

From a bucket standpoint, the key question is whether the payment is really compensation in disguise. If the employer is essentially just paying you more and labeling it "housing allowance," the IRS may still treat it as compensation. If it's a true reimbursement arrangement with tight documentation, it may be handled differently.

The danger is assuming the label on the payslip is the tax label. International payroll systems can be wonderfully creative with names. The IRS is far less impressed by creativity than by substance.

Interest and dividends: the portfolio bucket, even if you "worked" for it emotionally

Interest and dividends don't care how hard you worked to build the savings that generated them. They are returns on capital, which puts them in the "portfolio" bucket. This bucket often behaves badly for expats—not because it's unfair, but because people expect it to behave like compensation.

Here's how the misunderstanding usually sounds: "I'm abroad, so my U.S. taxes should be low." Then they realize a large portion of their annual cash flow is dividends from U.S. funds, interest from U.S. accounts, or distributions from investments that don't become magically foreign just because the investor moved.

This bucket is also where foreign taxes can be unpredictable. Some countries tax dividends heavily, others lightly. Withholding may occur at the source, and the paperwork you receive might not resemble U.S. forms. Meanwhile, the U.S. return may still want the items categorized (qualified vs nonqualified dividends, for example) in ways your foreign statements never mention.

A useful personal finance truth: you can live a fully international life and still have a very U.S.-centered portfolio. Your address doesn't automatically relocate the payers.

Capital gains: not a paycheck, even if it funds your year

If you sell investments to pay for life abroad—especially if you're taking a sabbatical or living off savings—the cash you withdraw can feel like "income." The IRS may see it as a capital transaction: proceeds minus basis, gain or loss, holding period, and so on.

The bucket problem is psychological: people classify by *purpose* ("this funds my rent") while the IRS classifies by *mechanics* ("this is a disposition of property"). Once you accept that difference, planning becomes clearer. Capital gains often interact with foreign tax credit strategies differently than wages do, and they can land in categories that don't play nicely with exclusions designed for compensation.

If you're living abroad on investment sales, your first-pass checklist should include: what was sold, when it was acquired, whether there were reinvested distributions that affect basis, and whether the brokerage reports basis correctly for your situation. The gain is often the taxable item, not the cash.

Rental income: a business-like bucket wearing a passive disguise

Rental property income sits in an awkward middle ground. It can feel passive ("tenants pay, I collect"), but the tax treatment looks more like running a small enterprise: gross rents, deductible expenses, depreciation, repairs versus improvements, and sometimes special rules depending on use.

The expat twist is that many people become accidental landlords. They move abroad, keep the U.S. home "just in case," and rent it out. Or they buy a place overseas and rent it when they travel. The bank deposits can look steady and simple, but the classification is not. Rental income has its own logic, and it can produce taxable income even in years where your cash flow feels tight, particularly when currency conversion and timing differences get involved.

Common trap: treating rent like a side-note and then being shocked when depreciation and expense categorization become central. Another trap: ignoring the currency mechanics. If rent is received in a foreign currency, you may need a consistent conversion approach for income and expenses. The bucket is "rental," not "salary," not "dividends," and that difference drives everything.

Royalties and licensing: the quiet cousin of freelancing and investing

If you earn money from intellectual property—book royalties, music streaming, software licenses, photo licensing—it can be easy to mis-bucket. It doesn't feel like wages, and it isn't a dividend, but it also might not feel like a "business" if it arrives without active work.

In practice, royalties often behave like their own category with distinctive sourcing and withholding patterns. A U.S. platform might issue a form; a foreign platform might issue nothing that resembles U.S. documentation. Withholding can be imposed by the payer's country, and treaties can affect rates. The key is to avoid tossing it into "miscellaneous income" and hoping the software figures it out. Label it clearly: royalty/licensing income, payer, country of payer, and what right was licensed.

Once it's labeled, you can determine whether it belongs on a business schedule, how to treat expenses, and how it interacts with credits and treaty positions.

Pensions, annuities, and retirement plan distributions: the "paid later" bucket

Retirement income is where expats often expect simplicity—"I already paid tax on this at some point"—and instead get a second education. Distributions from pensions, annuities, and retirement plans are typically not treated as compensation for current services. They're their own bucket with their own sourcing concepts, treaty overlays, and sometimes mismatches between countries about what is taxable and when.

This bucket is also where terminology causes expensive confusion. People refer to "my pension" when they mean a 401(k), or "my IRA" when they mean a foreign retirement account, or "my retirement account" when it's actually a taxable brokerage account earmarked for retirement. The IRS doesn't grade on intention. A distribution from a retirement plan is treated as a distribution from that plan, with rules attached.

Practical takeaway: whenever you see the word "distribution," slow down. Identify the plan type, the country where the plan is established, and whether the payment is a periodic pension-like stream or a lump sum. That single classification choice often dictates whether foreign taxes can be credited, whether treaty articles might be relevant, and what reporting forms may appear.

Social Security: familiar, but still its own category

Social Security benefits don't slot neatly into the same mental boxes as wages or pensions, and they come with their own U.S. tax rules. Abroad, they can also be treated very differently depending on local law and treaty provisions. The bucket label here isn't "retirement" in the generic sense—it's "Social Security benefits," which signals that the U.S. return will treat them under a distinct formula.

Even when Social Security is only a small slice of the household cash flow, misclassifying it as a pension distribution or as "other income" can cause incorrect results.

The "same bank account" problem: why commingling hides classification errors

Even if you understand buckets intellectually, day-to-day life tries to undo that understanding. Many expats simplify finances by routing everything through one account: salary, investment income, rent, reimbursements. It's convenient, but it trains your brain to think the account statement is a tax statement. It isn't.

Two habits help:

- Keep a simple ledger (spreadsheet is fine) that lists each inflow with a column for bucket label: wages, self-employed business receipts, interest, dividends, capital gains, rent, retirement distributions, Social Security, royalties, other.
- Attach "source documents" to the ledger: payslips, invoices, brokerage statements, rent summaries, pension statements, and any foreign withholding documents.

This isn't about turning your life into accounting homework. It's about reducing the year-end panic where you can't remember whether a payment was reimbursement for flights or a bonus, whether a dividend was from a U.S. fund or a foreign corporation, or whether that "distribution" was a sale of shares or a retirement withdrawal.

The classic traps expats hit when buckets are wrong

Mis-bucketing tends to produce the same set of headaches, over and over:

"All overseas money qualifies for the FEIE." The exclusion is built around compensation for services and a qualifying fact pattern. Dividends, interest, capital gains, rent, pensions, and most other portfolio/retirement items do not magically become excludable because you live abroad.

"Dividends are just like salary because they show up every quarter." Regularity does not turn a return on capital into pay. A dividend can be dependable, but it's still a portfolio item with its own treatment.

"My freelance work is basically the same as my job was." The work might be identical; the tax plumbing is not. Business income brings expense treatment, profit calculation, and often additional layers that employees never see.

"My bonus is foreign because I was living abroad when it hit." Timing in your bank account is not the same as where the underlying services happened.

"A retirement withdrawal is just money I saved." A retirement distribution is typically governed by the plan's rules. The origin of the money matters more than your emotional story about it.

When you hear yourself using words like "basically," "pretty much," or "it's all the same," that's usually a sign you're about to throw two different buckets into one.

A quick self-audit: label first, optimize second

Before you touch exclusions, credits, or treaty positions, it helps to do a "labeling pass" over your year:

- What did you receive because you worked (employee compensation)?
- What did you receive because you ran a business or did contract work (self-employed receipts)?
- What did you receive because you owned assets (interest, dividends, gains, rent, royalties)?
- What did you receive because past work is now paying you (pensions, retirement distributions, Social Security)?

Then add two notes next to each item: (1) the payer and (2) the dates or period it relates to. Those notes sound mundane, but they're often what prevents you from blending categories later when you're trying to coordinate relief from double taxation.

Once the buckets are correct, strategy becomes less like guessing and more like engineering. The U.S. system isn't necessarily friendly, but it is surprisingly consistent about one thing: it wants to know what kind of money you're talking about before it decides how to tax it.

2.2 What Makes Income US-Source or Foreign-Source

"Source" sounds like something a barista would ask about your beans. In U.S. tax terms, it's more like a GPS coordinate the IRS attaches to each type of income: *this dollar is considered to come from the United States* or *this dollar is considered to come from outside it.* That coordinate doesn't care where your bank account sits, what currency you were paid in, or how international your life feels. It follows rule sets that can be unintuitive—but once you learn the patterns, a lot of mysterious outcomes start making perfect sense.

Sourcing matters because the Foreign Tax Credit isn't just a "taxes paid overseas" coupon. Publication 514 ties the allowable credit to *foreign-source taxable income*. If you paid tax to a non-U.S. government on something the U.S. treats as U.S.-source, the credit may be limited or unusable. That's not moral judgment; it's architecture. The credit is designed to relieve double taxation on foreign-source income, so the IRS first demands: "Show me the foreign-source part."

The easiest way to get this right is to keep asking the two questions that stop almost every expat mistake mid-flight: *What type of income is it?* and *What is its source under U.S. rules?* Type comes first, because source rules are type-specific. Salary and dividends don't just have different tax rates—they have different sourcing logic.

The most misunderstood sourcing rule: for work, the map is your body

For compensation from working—whether you're an employee or a contractor—the U.S. sourcing rule is surprisingly physical. Services income is generally sourced to *where the services are performed*. Not where you were hired. Not where the company is headquartered. Not where the invoice was paid from. Not the country code in the payer's bank account.

This is why remote work can be both liberating and administratively annoying: your laptop becomes a location-dependent income machine. If you perform services while you're in Spain, that compensation is typically foreign-source. If you perform services while you're in the U.S., that portion is typically U.S.-source—even if the employer is foreign, even if your "official" job is abroad, even if you spent 340 days of the year outside the U.S.

It's also why vague language like "I work for a U.S. company" is close to meaningless for sourcing. The payer's identity is often not the deciding factor for personal services income. The deciding factor is where *you* were when you did the work.

That physical rule can feel almost quaint in a world of VPNs and virtual offices, but it's practical from the IRS's point of view. A day can be placed on a calendar. A flight can be documented. A passport stamp can exist. The IRS knows people can argue about "where the job is," so it anchors the rule to "where the worker was."

A concrete example: the France-based employee with a U.S. work sprint

Imagine you live in France and work for a French subsidiary of a multinational. Most of the year, you work in France. But the company flies you to New York for a project: 25 workdays in the U.S. You do real work there—meetings, deliverables, the full corporate experience—then you return to France.

Under the general idea in IRS guidance, when services are performed partly in and partly outside the U.S., the correct sourcing method is facts-and-circumstances; a day-count allocation is commonly used in practice and is explicitly described in IRS guidance for personal service income. In plain English: you can allocate your compensation based on workdays.

If you worked 25 days in the U.S. and 225 days abroad (250 total workdays for the year, for example), then 10% of that compensation would be U.S.-source and 90% foreign-source using a workday approach. That doesn't mean your employer will automatically withhold correctly, or that your French tax bill will neatly split the same way. It means that for U.S. purposes, you shouldn't treat the entire salary as foreign-source just because your life is centered in France.

This one allocation can echo through everything else:

- The portion of compensation attributable to U.S. workdays may not play nicely with a strategy that assumes all wages are foreign-source.

- The foreign tax credit limitation can change because the fraction of your taxable income that is "foreign-source" changes.
- If foreign taxes were imposed on the full salary (including the U.S.-work portion), you can end up with foreign tax paid on U.S.-source income—exactly the mismatch that causes credit limitation headaches.

The emotional trap here is that 25 workdays feels like "just a trip." The sourcing rule treats it as what it is: labor performed in the United States.

Freelancer paid by a U.S. client: the check's passport doesn't matter

Now take a freelancer in Portugal building software for a U.S. startup. The startup pays from a U.S. bank account, in dollars, with a contract governed by California law. The freelancer never sets foot in the U.S. all year.

Many people instinctively label this "U.S. income" because everything about the client relationship feels American. Sourcing rules for services income push back: the payer's location, payment location, and contract location generally do not control sourcing for personal services. Where the services are performed does.

So if the freelancer does all the work physically in Portugal, the compensation is generally foreign-source. That's true even though the client is U.S.-based and the money originates in the U.S. banking system. The IRS is not trying to claim every dollar that touches a U.S. company; it's applying a category rule: services performed abroad typically create foreign-source compensation.

This distinction is more than trivia. It affects how you think about foreign tax credits, local withholding, and what you can reasonably document. A U.S. payer may issue forms or reporting that makes the income feel "U.S." in flavor. The sourcing rules aren't interested in flavor; they're interested in location of performance.

Why "where I live" is not the same as "source"

People often assume source is a synonym for residence: "I live in Germany, therefore my income is German-source." Sometimes that's close enough, especially when your income is mostly salary for work physically done in Germany. But the similarity is accidental, not guaranteed.

Source is an attribute of *income items*. Residence is an attribute of *people*. A person can live abroad while receiving U.S.-source interest, U.S.-source dividends, U.S.-source rental income, or U.S.-source compensation for workdays spent in the U.S. That's how two expats with the same annual cash inflow can have very different U.S. outcomes: one is funded by foreign-source salary; the other is funded by a portfolio that remains U.S.-centered.

The practical mindset shift: stop asking "Where am I based?" as the first question. Ask "What is this payment, and what sourcing rule applies to that type?"

Interest: usually sourced to the payer

Once you leave services income, the sourcing rules become less physical and more about who is on the other side of the payment. Interest is the classic example. Interest is typically sourced based on the residence of the payer (in broad terms: who owes the debt). That means interest from a U.S. bank account can be U.S.-source even if you're living abroad and haven't visited the U.S. in years. Meanwhile, interest paid by a non-U.S. bank can be foreign-source even if you manage the account from your childhood bedroom in Ohio.

This is why "I'm abroad, so my investment income is foreign" can be wildly wrong. If your savings remain in U.S. institutions, your interest income often remains U.S.-source. That can matter for the foreign tax credit because foreign withholding or taxation on that interest might not translate into a usable U.S. credit the way you expect.

If you only remember one thing about sourcing for portfolio income, make it this: the "place where you clicked the button" is not the place the income is sourced.

Dividends: usually sourced to the corporation paying them, with odd exceptions

Dividends often follow a similar "who paid it" intuition: generally, dividends are sourced by reference to the corporation paying the dividend. That can make dividends from a U.S. corporation U.S.-source, and dividends from a foreign corporation foreign-source.

But dividends are also where expats get ambushed by structure. Many people don't own "foreign stocks" or "U.S. stocks" in a clean way; they own funds, ETFs, ADRs, and accounts that wrap one thing in another. The dividend statement you see might not make it obvious what the underlying payer really is.

There are also exceptions in the broader rule set that can make sourcing less intuitive in edge cases, which is exactly why treating dividends like wages ("I received it while abroad, so it's foreign") is such a reliable way to get burned. Dividends don't care where you were sitting when they were declared. They care about the identity and attributes of the payer.

When foreign taxes are withheld on dividends that are U.S.-source under U.S. rules, you can run into the same mismatch problem: real foreign tax paid, but limited ability to use it as a credit because the income isn't treated as foreign-source.

Capital gains: the seller's "tax home" enters the chat

Capital gains are where sourcing becomes a little philosophical. When you sell personal property like stock, what country is the gain "from"? The company is global, the exchange is electronic, and the buyer is anonymous. The U.S. has to pick a principle.

One key statutory anchor here is IRC §865, which establishes source rules for personal property sales and includes exceptions and anti-abuse rules. The broad idea most expats encounter is that the sale of personal property is generally sourced by the seller's tax home (subject to exceptions). In other words: your gain may be sourced with reference to where *you* are considered to have your tax home under the relevant framework, not where the company is headquartered and not where your brokerage sits.

This is a very different flavor from interest and dividends. For portfolio income like dividends, the payer's identity dominates. For capital gains on stock, the rule set can lean toward the seller's circumstances.

That doesn't mean capital gains are automatically foreign-source when you live abroad. "Tax home" is a term with specific meaning, and exceptions can matter. It does mean that capital gains sourcing can interact with the set of facts that establish your tax home, which is why sourcing and residency concepts often end up holding hands.

A practical note: because §865 is a framework with exceptions, and because countries often tax gains differently, capital gains are a common place where people pay foreign tax and then discover that the U.S. categorizes and sources the gain in a way that changes whether the Foreign Tax Credit is available or limited.

Rental income: usually tied to where the property sits

Rental income tends to feel intuitively sourceable because the property has an address. That intuition is usually your friend.

Real property doesn't travel. A rental in Texas is in Texas; a rental in Tokyo is in Tokyo. In sourcing terms, rental income is generally associated with the location of the property.

This is one reason expats who keep a U.S. home as a rental can find their U.S. return stays complicated even if their day job is entirely abroad. A U.S. rental tends to remain U.S.-source. If you pay tax abroad on that U.S. rental (which can happen depending on residence-based taxation in your country of residence), you can end up with foreign taxes on U.S.-source income—again raising credit limitation issues.

If you own overseas rentals, the reverse can be true: foreign-source rents with potential foreign taxes, and U.S. reporting obligations that still exist because, as you already know, worldwide reporting doesn't stop at the border.

Why sourcing is the engine room of Foreign Tax Credit planning

The Foreign Tax Credit limitation is where sourcing stops being an academic exercise and becomes a dollars-and-cents issue. Publication 514 ties the limitation to foreign-source taxable income. If you mis-source your income—say, you treat U.S.-source interest as foreign-source because you live abroad—you may overstate the portion of your income that supports a credit. That can lead to a credit that looks fine in April and looks like a problem later.

It also interacts with the "baskets" concept in the credit regime. Form 1116 often requires separate computations for different categories of income, and sourcing can determine which items go into which computation. When people say "the FTC didn't work for me," what they often mean is: "I had foreign taxes, but my U.S. return didn't have enough foreign-source taxable income in the relevant category to absorb the credit."

There's a special kind of frustration here because it feels unfair: you did pay foreign tax. The U.S. is not denying that. It's saying, "You paid foreign tax on something we don't treat as foreign-source, or you mixed categories." Once you see that as a mechanical limitation rather than a personal affront, the problem becomes solvable: you improve classification, improve sourcing, and then the credit computation starts behaving.

Remote work: the modern sourcing stress test

Remote work creates a new type of sourcing confusion: people conflate *employment relationship* with *place of performance*. They'll say, "My job is in the U.S." when they mean "My employer is in the U.S." Or they'll say, "I'm employed abroad" when they mean "I have a local contract."

Sourcing doesn't care about HR paperwork nearly as much as it cares about where the work was actually performed. That makes travel calendars suddenly important. A few weeks in the U.S. can change the sourcing of compensation. A "digital nomad" year with many countries can create a patchwork of foreign-source wages by country for local purposes, while U.S. sourcing focuses on whether any services were performed in the U.S. at all, and how much.

If you're mobile, the simplest discipline is to treat your workdays like a ledger, not a memory. Track where you were when you worked, not where you slept. A day spent answering emails from a U.S. airport lounge is still a day of services performed in the U.S. if you're doing substantive work there.

A fast way to sanity-check sourcing: ignore money movement and focus on the "driver"

When you're stuck, stop staring at where the cash came from and ask what the income is paying you *for*:

- If it's paying for your labor, the driver is usually *place of performance*.

- If it's paying you because someone owes you interest, the driver is often *who the payer is.*
- If it's paying you because you own stock, the driver is often *who the dividend-paying corporation is.*
- If it's paying you because you sold an asset, the driver may be *seller-based rules* (with §865 as a key anchor for personal property sales).
- If it's paying you because you own real estate, the driver is usually *location of the property.*

This isn't meant to replace professional advice in complex cases. It's meant to prevent the most common self-inflicted wound: assuming the source follows your mailing address or your employer's headquarters.

Two expats, same cash, different sourcing: why outcomes diverge

Picture two Americans living in the same city abroad. Each has $120,000 landing in their accounts over the year.

One earns $120,000 as salary for work performed entirely outside the U.S. The other has $60,000 salary abroad and $60,000 in dividends and interest from U.S. accounts and funds.

Even if both pay a similar amount of foreign tax, their U.S. outcomes can diverge sharply. The first person may have a large share of income that is foreign-source under the compensation rules. The second person may have a chunk of income that remains U.S.-source because portfolio sourcing tends to point back to the payer or issuer. When they go to compute credits, the second person can find themselves "short" on foreign-source income to support the credit, especially if foreign taxes are being charged on U.S.-source investment income under the rules of their country of residence.

They didn't do anything wrong. They just had different kinds of income, and different sourcing drivers. The IRS is not asking,

"Where do you live?" It's asking, "Where did this item come from under the rule for its category?"

The habit that keeps sourcing from turning into a year-end crisis

Sourcing problems are usually born in April, but conceived in September—when travel is busy, when work is hectic, when you're not thinking about your tax return at all. The way out is simple enough to fit in a notes app:

- For services income: keep a workday calendar with U.S. workdays clearly marked.
- For investment income: keep a list of accounts and payers (bank, broker, fund family) so you can identify whether the payer is U.S. or non-U.S.
- For asset sales: retain trade confirmations and basic holding details; if large gains are involved, flag that §865 may be relevant and that "seller/tax home" concepts can matter.
- For real estate: keep the property location and rental statements organized by property, not by bank account.

That's not busywork. It's the difference between a return that flows and a return that becomes a late-night detective novel with missing pages.

Sourcing is the quiet referee behind many expat-friendly provisions. If you treat it as a separate, deliberate step—type first, source second—you stop asking the tax software to guess what you meant. You tell it what actually happened. And the IRS, for all its quirks, responds surprisingly well to that kind of clarity.

2.3 Foreign Tax Residency and Why It Matters

You can live somewhere, love it, even learn to argue with your plumber in the local language—and still not be a "tax resident" there. Or you can be a tax resident without feeling particularly settled, the way many people do on year-long assignments that turn into three-year assignments that turn into "we should probably buy a sofa."

That gap between *life resident* and *tax resident* is where a lot of overseas filing drama is born. Countries don't tax you because you posted sunsets on Instagram; they tax you because you tripped their domestic residency rules. Those rules are local-law creatures: built for that country's politics, budget needs, and ideas about fairness. They can be simple ("183 days") or maddeningly holistic ("center of vital interests"), and they can produce outcomes that feel personal even when they're purely administrative.

Foreign tax residency matters because it decides three high-stakes questions in your day-to-day reality:

- Do you have to file a local return, even if nothing was withheld?
- Does the country tax only local-source items, or your worldwide income?
- Can you access treaty benefits and documentation that make cross-border taxation less painful?

The U.S. will still want its paperwork and calculations either way. The difference is whether your host country also claims a comprehensive right to tax you—and whether you can prove, on paper, what your status is.

Tax residency is not a vibe; it's a trigger

A surprising number of expats operate on a "common sense" model: "I'm on a work visa, so I must be a tax resident," or "I'm renting month-to-month, so I can't be a resident." Common sense is not the governing law.

Many countries use a day-count test as a blunt instrument, but it's rarely the only instrument. Some add a "permanent home" concept. Some care where your spouse and kids live. Some look at where you habitually work, where your economic life is anchored, or whether you've cut ties to your former country. Some countries treat you as resident from the moment you arrive with an intent to stay; others treat you as resident only after a threshold is crossed. A few have split-year rules that can feel like a tax version of jet lag: resident for part of the year, nonresident for the rest.

The important point isn't memorizing every country's test. It's accepting that "residency" is something you can accidentally trigger, and it often triggers retroactively for the year. If you wait until the following spring to find out whether you were resident, you've already lost the ability to plan cleanly.

The practical consequences: filing, rates, and what gets taxed

Foreign tax residency often changes the size and shape of your local obligations more than any single planning technique ever will.

A nonresident in many jurisdictions is taxed on local-source items (salary for local work, local rentals, local business income) and may have simplified withholding. A resident is often taxed on worldwide income, may need to report foreign accounts or foreign investments locally, and may be pulled into higher or more progressive tax brackets. Some systems offer generous exclusions or remittance-style rules for newcomers; others flip the "worldwide" switch immediately.

For Americans abroad, the sting is that "worldwide" usually means the same familiar list you report to the U.S.: dividends, interest, capital gains, retirement distributions, and sometimes even things you thought were purely U.S.-based. That can create real double-tax pressure—especially when the host country taxes items the U.S. taxes preferentially, or taxes them at different times.

This is why residency abroad isn't simply a question of "Where do I pay?" It's "Who gets first claim, and on what categories?"

Foreign residency can strengthen your U.S. strategy—even when it increases local obligations

Becoming tax-resident abroad can feel like stepping into a brighter spotlight: more forms, more reporting, more chances to get something wrong. But it also can bring benefits that are quietly powerful.

First, it can make local taxation more predictable. If you're clearly resident, you can often access local deductions, credits, family allowances, and filing statuses that a nonresident can't. Second, it can improve your ability to document what happened. Foreign tax paid—properly assessed, properly reported—tends to be easier to defend than ad hoc withholding with no return filed. Third, residency can matter for treaty benefits and for obtaining paperwork that U.S. processes sometimes implicitly depend on.

The tension is real: local residency can increase your exposure, but it can also give you the documentation and legal footing to coordinate U.S. relief mechanisms in a way that's less guessy. That coordination doesn't happen automatically, but it becomes possible.

A key distinction: bona fide residence (U.S. concept) vs tax residency (local concept)

Americans often hear the word "residence" and assume it's one universal status. It isn't. "Bona fide residence" for purposes of FEIE is a U.S. tax concept with its own criteria. Treasury regulations indicate it is determined by applying (to the extent practical) principles used for determining residence of aliens under §871—meaning it's a facts-and-circumstances style determination rather than purely a day-count exercise.

That single sentence is worth sitting with because it explains a lot of confusion:

- You can be a bona fide resident abroad under U.S. rules while living in a place with little or no tax, because the U.S. test is about your living pattern and connection, not whether the host country billed you.
- You can be a tax resident abroad under local law and still fail the U.S. "bona fide residence" framework if your facts don't support a genuine move of your life abroad.

People sometimes try to borrow the host country's residency certificate as a magic shield ("See, I'm resident there!") or, conversely, try to use the absence of local tax as proof they're not settled abroad ("They don't tax me, so I must not be resident!"). Both moves confuse two different systems.

Foreign tax residency answers: "What does this country consider you for its own tax purposes?" Bona fide residence answers a different question: "Does the U.S. regard your overseas life as sufficiently established for its own statutory benefit tests?" They can align, but neither controls the other.

The no-tax-jurisdiction reality check: when credits disappear, but FEIE may still exist

Some expats live in places where personal tax is minimal or nonexistent—an oil-economy style jurisdiction, a territorial system, or a special regime for certain residents. This creates a planning fork that people often don't see coming.

If you pay little or nothing locally, the Foreign Tax Credit becomes less useful simply because there is little foreign tax to credit. That doesn't prevent FEIE eligibility by itself; FEIE is not conditioned on paying foreign tax. But the absence of local tax changes how you think about the rest of your income picture: investment income, self-employment profit, retirement distributions, and any compensation that doesn't fit neatly into exclusion mechanics.

It also changes your risk profile. In high-tax countries, many U.S. taxpayers can lean on credits as a pressure valve for double taxation. In low-tax jurisdictions, you can still have a full U.S. tax bill on anything not sheltered by exclusions, deductions, or favorable rates. The emotional experience is different: you don't feel "double-taxed," but you can feel like you're not getting any "expat advantage" either.

Foreign residency still matters in this scenario because it can affect whether the host country taxes anything at all, what local filings are required, and whether you can obtain official documentation of status when treaty or withholding questions arise.

Treaties: not a blanket exemption, but a set of targeted knobs

Tax treaties are the part of international tax that people most want to believe in and least want to read. The popular version is: "There's a treaty, so I don't pay U.S. tax." The reality is fussier and more useful.

Publication 901 is the IRS's consumer-facing gateway to treaty concepts. The big idea it helps communicate is that treaties operate by *country* and *income type*. A treaty is not a global coupon; it's a negotiated list of rules: how dividends are taxed, how pensions are taxed, what happens with dependent personal services, and so on. Some articles reduce withholding rates. Some clarify residency tie-breakers. Some prevent certain kinds of double taxation. Many do nothing for U.S. citizens on certain categories because of how treaties are drafted.

Foreign tax residency is often a prerequisite to even claim treaty benefits in the other country. Many treaty benefits are available only to a "resident" of a contracting state as defined by the treaty. That treaty definition usually leans on local law residency first, then uses tie-breaker rules if both countries claim you. So when you hear "to claim treaty benefits you may need a certificate of residence," that's not bureaucracy for sport. It's how the treaty system establishes who is allowed to claim the deal.

This is where the paperwork starts to matter as much as the rules. Foreign tax residency (local law) can matter for what documents you can obtain—tax residence certificates—and those documents can influence withholding tax outcomes and benefit eligibility in many contexts.

Tie-breakers: when two countries both say "you're ours"

Some situations create a strange kind of tax tug-of-war: you meet the residency definition in two places at the same time. This can happen when you move mid-year, maintain homes, split your time, or have family ties pulling in a different direction than your job.

Treaties often include "tie-breaker" rules to resolve dual residency for treaty purposes: concepts like permanent home, center of vital interests, habitual abode, and sometimes citizenship as a final decider. The details vary by treaty, but the theme is the same: the treaty tries to assign you to one country as your "treaty resident" so the two systems can stop fighting over the same income categories.

This matters enormously for non-citizens who are U.S. residents under domestic law—especially green card holders and others who might be resident under U.S. tests but also resident elsewhere. Treaty residency and treaty tie-breakers can alter U.S. tax treatment for non-citizens who would otherwise be U.S. residents under the green card test or substantial presence test; Publication 519 flags this and references disclosure requirements.

That last clause—*disclosure requirements*—is not decorative. Claiming a treaty position can trigger additional reporting, and failing to disclose can be its own problem even if the underlying position is correct. The exact mechanism varies with the claim, but the habit is consistent: if you're taking a treaty-based position that changes your U.S. classification or taxation, treat it like a formal stance, not a casual assumption. Publication 519's reference to Form 8833 is a clue that the IRS expects transparency about certain treaty claims.

Withholding: where tax residency quietly moves real money

A lot of treaty and residency issues show up not as philosophical debates but as withholding on a statement.

Dividends are a great example. If you're resident in a country with a treaty that reduces dividend withholding, the payer (or broker) may apply a lower withholding rate—*if* you can certify your residency appropriately. Without that certification, you might be withheld at a default or statutory rate. The difference can be large, and it can persist year after year because nobody wants to reopen the file.

The same principle applies to pensions, royalties, and other cross-border payments. Residency determines what rate a payer applies, and treaties often determine whether the rate is reduced. If you can't prove residency, you may not get the reduction. If you can prove residency but you misunderstand what the treaty covers, you might get the reduction and later discover it wasn't appropriate.

Foreign tax residency (local law) matters here because it affects withholding tax outcomes in the realest sense: cash not withheld is cash you don't have to wait to recover through a refund process.

Residency and the "shape" of double taxation

Not all double taxation feels the same. Sometimes the same income is taxed by two countries, but one gives a credit or exemption that prevents the double bite. Sometimes the double bite happens anyway because the two systems disagree on:

- *Timing*: one country taxes when the income is earned; the other taxes when it's paid or realized.
- *Character*: one country calls it a capital gain; the other calls it ordinary income.
- *Residence*: one country taxes worldwide income because you are resident; the other taxes because of citizenship or source.

Foreign tax residency sits right in the middle of that. If you are resident abroad and that country taxes worldwide income, then your U.S.-reported categories (salary, dividends, capital gains, retirement) can become locally taxable too. That can create the need for credits, and it can make sourcing and categorization—already discussed—feel suddenly urgent.

On the other hand, if you are *not* resident abroad, you may be taxed locally only on local-source items. That might reduce foreign taxes paid (and therefore reduce credits available), but it can also reduce complexity. Some expats choose arrangements that keep them nonresident in the host country specifically to avoid worldwide local taxation. That choice can be sensible, but it should be deliberate, because "nonresident" often comes with its own limitations and vulnerabilities.

A year-end checklist mindset that prevents residency surprises

Residency is one of those things where the cleanest planning happens before December, and the messiest happens after you've already crossed the threshold.

The most practical approach is to treat foreign tax residency as something you monitor, not something you discover. That means knowing, early, what the trigger is in your country and how close you are to it. It also means understanding whether your country uses a day-count test alone or combines it with a "home" or "center of life" test that can override day counting.

Even if your country does use a simple day-count rule, don't assume days are obvious. Travel days, partial days, transit, and what counts as "presence" can differ. If you're close to a threshold, keep records that are better than memory: flight itineraries, passport stamps, and a simple calendar that distinguishes travel days from workdays.

This is where many expats discover that "I'm not sure" is an expensive answer. If you don't know whether you are locally resident, you don't know whether you should have filed. If you don't know whether you should have filed, you don't know whether your foreign tax was computed correctly. And if your foreign tax isn't computed correctly, the U.S. side of the coordination gets shakier.

The punchline: residency is the permission slip for an entire tax system

Foreign tax residency is not merely a label you put on a form. It's a country deciding whether it gets to treat you like a full member of its tax system. That decision affects rates, filings, documentation, and treaty access. It can make double taxation more likely in raw terms (because more of your income becomes locally taxable), while simultaneously making relief mechanisms more workable (because the local system is now formally engaged and documentable).

Handled casually, residency becomes a surprise bill and a paperwork spiral. Handled deliberately, it becomes a known constraint—like weather you plan around—so your U.S. strategy is built on solid ground rather than guesses about what the host country "probably" considers you.

The easiest way to stay out of trouble is almost boring: learn the host country's residency trigger, track it during the year, and collect whatever local documentation you'll need if withholding, treaty rates, or credit claims depend on proving where you're resident. That boring discipline is what turns cross-border tax from a recurring emergency into a manageable system.

2.4 Tax Home, Abode, and the Facts That Support Your Position

The IRS doesn't audit your feelings. It audits your facts.

That sounds harsh until you realize it's also fair: "I meant to move abroad" is not a tax position. "I was living and working abroad, and here is the record that proves it" is. The difference between those two sentences is often the difference between a smooth FEIE claim and a letter you'd rather not receive.

Two terms do most of the heavy lifting here: *tax home* and *abode*. They're easy to confuse because they sound like synonyms for "where you live." Under U.S. rules, they're not. They're closer to competing biographies of your year: one about where your work life is centered, the other about where your personal life is anchored.

If you treat them as paperwork vocabulary, you'll miss the point. They're really a standards-of-proof problem: what story do your actions tell?

Tax home: your work's headquarters, not your favorite address

Tax home for §911 generally tracks the regular/principal place of business. That's the regulatory framing, and it's delightfully blunt: where do you actually do your work? Where is your professional life based? For most people, that's a specific city and country. For others—consultants, flight crews, rotating assignment workers—it's messier.

Form 2555 instructions operationalize this in a way that surprises many expats: tax home isn't necessarily your family home; it is usually where you work. If you take nothing else from the concept, take that. A house you own, a bedroom you keep at your parents' place, a mailing address you maintain for convenience—none of those automatically controls your tax home. The gravitational center of your work does.

This is why someone can keep a U.S. address for banking and still have a foreign tax home if their regular/principal place of business is abroad. It's also why someone can spend a lot of nights abroad and still fail the tax-home analysis if their working life never really leaves the U.S.

When a person has no regular or principal place of business—because the work is truly itinerant—tax home can become the regular place of abode in a real and substantial sense. That phrase sounds philosophical, but it's basically the IRS saying: "If you don't have a work base, we'll look for a life base." Which brings us to the concept that trips people more often than day counts: abode.

Abode: where your life is, in the unromantic sense

Abode is not "where you sleep." It's "where your personal, family, and economic ties are strongest"—where your life is actually centered. Case law (including cases often cited in this area such as Jones and Acone) underscores that abode is evaluated via ties and life-center facts, not just travel logs. Courts look at where family lives, where personal and economic ties are strongest, and why the taxpayer is abroad.

This is where the "I met the day count" mindset breaks down. You can have an overseas work contract, rack up plenty of days outside the U.S., and still have an abode problem if your life infrastructure remains U.S.-centered: spouse and kids at home in the States, a U.S. house kept available for your use, U.S. clubs and doctors and bank branches and voting patterns, a revolving-door travel schedule that always circles back to the same American nest.

The statutory sting is direct: even if work location suggests a foreign tax home, §911 denies foreign tax home treatment for periods when the taxpayer's abode is in the United States (with narrow exceptions not relevant to most readers). In other words, you don't get to say "my tax home is abroad" if the overall facts show your abode never really moved.

This is why "abode" matters so much. It's the IRS's way of preventing a purely logistical interpretation of working abroad. The rule is trying to distinguish between (a) a person who has genuinely shifted their life abroad and (b) a person who is temporarily offshore while their life remains U.S.-based.

The most common pitfall: the split-life arrangement

The most common pitfall pattern for general audiences is attempting to claim FEIE by meeting day counts while keeping significant U.S.-centered personal/family ties and infrastructure—creating an "abode in the U.S." problem.

Here's a fact pattern that shows up in real life because it's emotionally sensible:

You take a long assignment overseas. You rent a place abroad. Your employer calls it an expat posting. But your spouse and children stay in the U.S. because school is good, or a parent needs care, or the family doesn't want the upheaval. You keep the U.S. home fully available; it's not rented out, because it's "still our home." You return frequently—birthdays, holidays, parent-teacher conferences, the occasional "I just need a week to breathe." The overseas apartment is functional, but it doesn't have much of your life in it. You're living out of two closets.

From a human perspective, that's a mature compromise. From an abode perspective, it can be dangerous. The facts may suggest your true home base—the place where family life, community, and long-term ties remain—is still the United States. In court decisions, that kind of tie pattern is exactly what gets scrutinized: why are you abroad, what is temporary, what is permanent, and where is the center of your personal and economic life?

A key point that surprises people: the IRS isn't required to be persuaded by your employer's narrative. "International assignment" is corporate language. The IRS is looking for the life pattern behind the language.

The contrasting pattern: the clean break (and why it's persuasive)

Now flip the fact pattern:

You move abroad and your family moves with you. You sign a long lease (or buy a home) overseas that looks like a place someone actually lives, not a crash pad. You sell the U.S. home or rent it out to an unrelated tenant so it's no longer sitting there waiting for you like a permanent landing strip. You move your daily financial life: local bank account for bills, local phone plan, local doctors, local routine. Your travel back to the U.S. becomes a visit rather than a commute.

This "clean break" isn't a moral achievement. It's simply a fact set that tells a consistent story: life moved. The stronger and more coherent your story is, the less you have to rely on technicalities.

Many expats resist this framing because it feels like the IRS is demanding a dramatic severance from the U.S. It's not. People can keep U.S. friendships, U.S. accounts, and U.S. assets. The question is whether the U.S. still looks like the center of your non-work life.

If your records show your work is abroad and your life is abroad, "tax home abroad" stops being an argument and becomes an observation.

Why the "available U.S. home" detail matters so much

One of the most telling facts in an abode analysis is whether you maintain a home in the U.S. that remains available for your personal use.

A U.S. home that is rented out to someone else (on a real lease) tends to read like an asset. A U.S. home kept empty "for when we're back" reads like a base. The IRS and courts tend to notice that difference because it signals intent and lifestyle. Keeping a home available often correlates with other U.S.-centered ties: family staying behind, frequent returns, U.S. memberships, U.S. day-to-day administration.

This doesn't mean you must sell your home to live abroad. It means you should understand the message your housing arrangements send. If you keep a U.S. home available and also claim your abode is abroad, you're asking your facts to tell two stories at once. Sometimes they can. Often they can't.

Itinerant work: when "no regular place of business" becomes its own scrutiny magnet

Some careers make "regular/principal place of business" hard to pin down. Think of a highly mobile contractor who bounces between client sites in multiple countries, or a project specialist who is always "on rotation." In those cases, tax home can become the regular place of abode in a real and substantial sense.

That sounds like a fallback that should help, but it also invites scrutiny because it raises the obvious question: if your work is everywhere, where is your life actually based? An itinerant lifestyle can look like "nowhere is home," and the IRS has historically been skeptical of "I have no home" narratives that conveniently produce the best tax result.

If you're in this category, the evidence you keep matters even more, because you'll be relying on a pattern rather than a single address. You want your record to show a real base abroad: long-term housing, local registration where applicable, consistent community ties, and travel patterns that look like departures from a base and returns to a base.

Without that, you can end up in an uncomfortable gray zone where you're arguing both that you're abroad and that you're not really anywhere—arguments that don't age well under examination.

The evidence mindset: build a file, not a memory

The best time to create evidence is when you don't need it. The worst time is when you're trying to reconstruct a year from photos, emails, and your calendar app's best guess at your location.

A useful way to think about the IRS's perspective is: if you had to prove your situation to someone who has never met you, what would you show them? The answer is not a passionate explanation. It's documents and patterns.

Here are categories of facts that often matter in tax home and abode disputes, and why they carry weight:

- *Work location and continuity*: contracts, assignment letters, work permits, and a consistent record of where work was performed. This supports the "regular/principal place of business" story.
- *Housing abroad*: leases, utility bills, local registrations, and evidence that the housing is truly used as a home (not just a hotel replacement).
- *Family location*: where spouse and children live and attend school is an especially strong indicator of abode. It's hard to argue your life center is abroad while your nuclear family's life is firmly in the U.S.
- *U.S. home status*: is it sold, rented, or sitting available? This single fact often shapes the credibility of the narrative.
- *Travel frequency and purpose*: patterns of travel back to the U.S. that look like "commuting to home" can undermine an overseas abode story. Purpose matters too: extended stays for family life look different than brief visits.
- *Economic and social ties*: where you bank for daily life, where your driver's license is maintained, where you participate in clubs or community life, and where your core financial affairs are managed. No single tie is decisive; the pattern is.

None of these items is magical. The IRS isn't checking boxes; it's weighing a story. But the more your documents align with one coherent story, the less room there is for doubt.

Day counts: useful, but not the whole case

Day counts still matter, especially for qualification tests that rely on physical presence. But day counts are often misused as a substitute for everything else: "I have my spreadsheet, therefore I'm safe."

A day-count spreadsheet is necessary for many people, but it's not sufficient to solve an abode problem. Think of it like a timecard: it proves where you were, not where your life is. Courts have made that distinction repeatedly in substance, even when taxpayers had extensive travel logs.

That doesn't mean you should keep a sloppy day record. Quite the opposite. A good travel record supports your sourcing allocations and keeps you honest about where work happened. Just don't let it become your only proof of living abroad.

Why you're abroad matters (and you should be prepared to explain it)

One detail that quietly affects credibility is *why* you're abroad. Are you there for a fixed project? Are you building a life? Are you there because your employer sent you, or because you relocated by choice? None of these is "better," but they create different expectations about ties.

If you are abroad on what is clearly a temporary project while everything personal remains in the U.S., the IRS may see a temporary work arrangement layered on top of an American abode. If you are abroad with a long-term pattern and have reorganized your life accordingly, your story reads differently.

When you keep records, keep the narrative pieces too: assignment dates, extensions, renewals, evidence of permanence (like longer leases or school enrollment). Not because the IRS wants your memoir, but because context makes the documents make sense.

A practical recordkeeping kit that doesn't take over your life

You don't need a color-coded binder with tabs. You need a light system you will actually maintain.

A workable approach for many expats is a digital folder for each tax year with subfolders like:

- *Travel*: itineraries, passport stamps (photos are fine), entry/exit records if available, and a simple calendar export.
- *Housing*: lease(s), renewals, utility bills, proof of local address registration.
- *Work*: contract/assignment letter, visa/work permit, employer letters that state work location.
- *Family and ties*: school enrollment, local insurance, local memberships, evidence of local life.
- *U.S. home*: rental lease if applicable, property management statements, or sale documents.

Add one tiny habit: once a month, drop your travel and housing proofs into the folder. Monthly beats annual because annual relies on memory, and memory is the least audit-friendly storage medium ever invented.

The core idea: your "position" is a pattern, not a form

People often talk about "taking" the FEIE or "using" a tax benefit as if it's a coupon you apply at checkout. In reality, you're asserting a set of facts: where you worked, where you lived, where your life was centered. Tax home and abode are the IRS's way of checking whether those facts hang together.

If your life is genuinely abroad, the proof usually exists naturally: leases, local registrations, routines, and a travel pattern that looks like visiting the U.S., not orbiting it. If your life is split, you can still be compliant, but you need to be realistic about how the IRS weighs ties—and you need to keep better records, because ambiguity attracts questions.

Tax rules can feel abstract, but tax home and abode are almost aggressively concrete. They live in the details of your calendar, your household, and your choices about what you kept in the U.S. “just in case.” The IRS can’t read your intent, but it can read your footprints. Keeping those footprints clear is one of the most quietly powerful things an expat can do.

Chapter 3

Using FEIE and Foreign Housing Effectively

For many Americans abroad, FEIE sounds like a magic eraser for US tax. It is not. Used well, it can shrink a tax bill dramatically; used casually, it can block credits, waste deductions, or create headaches when life changes. This chapter helps readers see FEIE as a strategy, not just a form.

3.1 What FEIE Can Exclude and When It Helps

The Foreign Earned Income Exclusion (FEIE) is a rare creature in the U.S. tax code: a benefit that can make a large chunk of income simply *not taxable* by the United States. Not reduced. Not deferred. Excluded. That one word is the hook—and also the trap. FEIE is powerful, but it is narrow by design, and it has a particular personality. Used in the right situation, it can turn a stressful April into a non-event. Used in the wrong situation, it can quietly waste other tax benefits, distort your planning, and leave you paying more than you needed to.

FEIE is not a "being overseas" prize. It is a "you performed services abroad" rule. Think of it as the IRS drawing a bright boundary around *earned* income—money that comes from your labor—and offering to ignore up to a statutory limit if you meet the qualification tests. That framing matters because expat finances often blend salary, bonuses, side gigs, investment accounts back home, a rental property you forgot counts as a business, and maybe an RSU vest that hits your paycheck like a meteor. FEIE only cares about the slice that is compensation for work you did outside the United States during a qualifying period, with a foreign tax home.

That means the first question isn't "Do I qualify?" It's "What do I actually have to exclude?" If your income is mostly portfolio returns, FEIE is like bringing a wrench to a software problem: impressive tool, wrong job. If your income is wages or self-employment income tied to services performed abroad, FEIE is suddenly the bluntest, fastest way to shrink your U.S. taxable income.

FEIE's sweet spot: compensation for personal services

The phrase *foreign earned income* sounds broad, like it might include anything you "earned" in the everyday sense. The tax meaning is tighter. It generally covers:

- wages and salary for work performed abroad,
- bonuses and other cash compensation tied to that work,
- professional fees (consulting, freelancing, contract work) for services performed abroad,
- certain allowances and noncash benefits that are treated as taxable compensation for U.S. purposes.

The unifying theme is that there's a human being doing labor. The IRS is not asking where your employer is headquartered or what currency you're paid in. It cares where *you* performed the services. If you're in Paris writing code for a U.S. company, your work is performed in France. If you fly to Chicago for two weeks of meetings, those two weeks are U.S.-performed services. That sourcing principle is the backbone of the whole FEIE story—and one reason frequent travel can turn "simple exclusion" into "calendar archaeology."

This is also why FEIE often feels most natural for people on straightforward pay arrangements: a single job, mostly performed outside the United States, paid as W-2 wages or the foreign equivalent, with no complicated deferrals and no equity compensation ping-ponging across borders. The more your compensation package resembles a clean salary, the more FEIE resembles a clean solution.

What FEIE does *not* touch (and why that matters)

FEIE's blind spot is passive income—money that comes from owning things rather than doing things. Dividends, interest, capital gains, rental profits, pension-type income, Social Security, annuities: these don't become "foreign earned" just because you read the brokerage statement while sitting in Lisbon.

This creates a common expat surprise: FEIE may wipe out U.S. tax on your paycheck, yet your U.S. return still has a pulse—and sometimes a bill—because your non-wage income is still fully in the game. A few examples that frequently catch people off guard:

- You exclude your salary, but you sold stock and triggered capital gains.
- Your salary is excluded, but your U.S. rental property throws off income.
- Your paycheck is excluded, but your savings account interest (however tiny) is still taxable and still must be reported.

None of this is a reason to avoid FEIE. It's a reason to stop thinking of FEIE as a universal eraser. If your financial life has multiple "income engines," FEIE may only turn off one of them.

The stacking rule: the exclusion isn't a rate cut

FEIE removes qualifying income from U.S. taxable income, but it does *not* politely pretend that income never existed when determining your tax bracket for the rest of your income. Under the "stacking" calculation, the IRS figures out what tax rate would apply if your excluded income were still there, then applies that higher rate to your remaining taxable income.

In plain English: FEIE can keep you from paying tax on your wages, but it won't necessarily keep your investment income (or other non-excludable income) in a low bracket. If you have significant non-wage income, FEIE may reduce the dollar amount subject to tax while still leaving the tax rate on the leftover dollars surprisingly high.

That's not an argument against claiming it. It's a warning about expectations. Many expats mentally model FEIE as "my income drops, so my bracket drops." With stacking, the bracket often doesn't drop the way you'd expect. The exclusion can still be extremely valuable; it just doesn't always deliver the psychological comfort of "I'm in a lower bracket now."

FEIE shines brightest in low-tax (or no-tax) countries

Here's the planning tension that runs through almost every expat return: the U.S. offers two major ways to reduce double taxation on earned income—excluding it (FEIE) or using a credit system based on taxes you paid to another country. The right tool depends heavily on your host country's tax rate.

FEIE tends to be a star in places where local income tax is low, where you receive special expat concessions, or where your compensation is structured in a way that keeps local tax modest. In those situations, you may not have enough local tax to offset much U.S. tax through credits. FEIE can step in and do what credits cannot: eliminate U.S. income tax on a big portion of wages even when the host country didn't tax them much.

A classic example is the expat in a jurisdiction with territorial taxation, tax holidays, or simply low rates on employment income.

Without FEIE, that person can end up with an honest-to-goodness U.S. tax bill on their wages despite having a perfectly compliant local tax life. With FEIE, the wage portion may disappear from U.S. income tax entirely (subject to the limit and the other rules).

In high-tax countries, FEIE can be useful—but not always the best first move

In higher-tax countries, many taxpayers have a different experience: they already pay enough host-country income tax that credits can wipe out most or all U.S. income tax on the same earnings. In that environment, FEIE's main advantage—excluding income—can be less valuable than it appears, and sometimes counterproductive.

Why? Because an exclusion and a credit are not additive on the same income. If you exclude wages, you generally can't also use credits on taxes attributable to those excluded wages in the same way; the tax system doesn't let you "double-dip" by eliminating the income and also claiming full relief for taxes paid on it. So FEIE can reduce the pool of income that would otherwise generate credit capacity.

That's where planning becomes less about heroically hunting the biggest deduction and more about managing constraints. In high-tax countries, the more interesting question is often: *Do I want to exclude income, or do I want to keep it taxable in the U.S. so that the credit mechanism has something to work with?* Sometimes the best answer is credits. Sometimes it's FEIE plus credits on other categories. Sometimes it's FEIE in one life phase and credits later. But "FEIE is always best because it's an exclusion" is a myth that high-tax expats learn to unlearn.

Who FEIE tends to help the most

FEIE's best use cases often share a few real-world characteristics. If you recognize yourself in these, FEIE is more likely to be a central part of your strategy:

You have clean earned income and not much else.

A teacher, engineer, nurse, consultant, or manager with a salary and a checking account is FEIE's home court. The return can be remarkably straightforward: exclude qualifying wages, report the rest, and you're done.

You're in a low-tax environment.

If the host country takes little or no income tax, FEIE can prevent the U.S. from becoming the "default tax home" for your wages.

You're early-career or mid-career with income under (or not far above) the FEIE limit.

FEIE is capped each year. If your compensation is within that cap (or close), FEIE can cover most or all of your earned income for U.S. income tax purposes. If your compensation is far above the cap, FEIE still helps, but it becomes a partial shield rather than a bunker.

Your goal is to reduce current U.S. income tax quickly and predictably.

FEIE is relatively direct: qualifying income goes out; taxable income goes down. Some other strategies feel more like chess. FEIE can feel more like turning off a faucet.

Who should pause before defaulting to FEIE

FEIE is sometimes claimed because it's famous, not because it's optimal. Certain profiles deserve a slower, more deliberate approach:

You're in a high-tax country and consistently owe zero U.S. income tax using credits.

If your current setup already neutralizes U.S. income tax, FEIE may offer little additional benefit and may reduce flexibility. The right move can still be FEIE in some cases, but it should be an intentional choice, not muscle memory.

You have meaningful investment income, capital gains, or rental income.

Remember stacking: excluding wages may not reduce the tax rate on your remaining income. In some cases, keeping wages in the U.S. tax calculation (and offsetting them with credits) can preserve a more favorable outcome for other income categories. The details matter, but the headline is simple: the more your return resembles a layered cake, the less likely one big exclusion solves everything neatly.

You're self-employed and expecting FEIE to erase everything.

FEIE can exclude qualifying self-employment income from *income tax*, but it does not automatically eliminate self-employment tax (Social Security and Medicare). Many self-employed expats are shocked to discover they can have "no taxable income" after FEIE and still owe substantial self-employment tax. Whether that applies depends on your situation, including any applicable social security agreements, but the key point is that FEIE is not a universal "no tax" button for the self-employed.

You have complex compensation timing (equity pay, deferred bonuses, multi-country workdays).

FEIE can still apply, but the sourcing and timing questions get sharper. Equity compensation, in particular, often spans grant dates, vest dates, and work performed in multiple places. FEIE doesn't become impossible here—it becomes a documentation and allocation exercise, and mistakes can be expensive.

FEIE as a planning tool, not a personality trait

A subtle trap is turning FEIE into an identity: "I'm an FEIE person." But the best expat tax strategies are situational. A move from Singapore to Germany can flip the value of FEIE versus credits. A promotion that pushes income above the exclusion limit changes the math. A spouse starts working, investments mature, a rental property is sold, you begin consulting on the side—suddenly the return is a different animal.

FEIE is also not a moral stance about taxation. It's a mechanical election with mechanical consequences. The smartest way to think about it is like choosing between two ways to relieve double taxation pressure: one removes income from the U.S. system; the other leaves income in but tries to neutralize the tax through credits. Your job is not to be loyal to one mechanism. Your job is to choose the mechanism that fits your income mix, your host country's tax bite, and your likely near-term future.

A few "surprisingly common" FEIE misconceptions

Some misunderstandings show up so frequently that they're worth disarming early—especially because they sound plausible at dinner parties.

"If my employer is American, my income can't be foreign."

Employer nationality doesn't decide sourcing. Where the work is performed is usually the key driver.

"If I'm paid in U.S. dollars into my U.S. bank, it's U.S. income."

Currency and bank location are not decisive. They may affect reporting and foreign account rules, but they don't dictate whether wages are foreign earned income.

"If I exclude my salary, I don't need to file."

FEIE is claimed *on* a U.S. return. The act of using it is part of filing.

"FEIE means I'm done with U.S. tax."

FEIE can zero out U.S. income tax on wages, but it doesn't erase filing obligations, it doesn't automatically shield other income types, and it doesn't automatically eliminate payroll-type taxes for self-employed individuals.

Each of these myths persists because it flatters a hope: that the rules are simpler than they are. The actual rules are still usable and navigable—they just require aiming FEIE at the right target.

The practical FEIE decision: what are you trying to protect?

A useful way to choose FEIE is to stop thinking in terms of "maximum exclusion" and instead think in terms of what you're protecting:

- If you're protecting *cash flow* in a low-tax jurisdiction, FEIE can be the main shield.
- If you're protecting *flexibility* across multiple income types and a high-tax jurisdiction already neutralizes U.S. tax, credits may be the sturdier framework.
- If you're protecting *simplicity* and your financial life is mostly wages, FEIE often provides an elegant reduction in complexity.

The best answer is frequently not ideological. It's pragmatic. And it starts with an honest inventory of your income types. Wages are the headline, but the "small" items—interest, dividends, a side consulting invoice, an RSU vest—are where FEIE's limitations suddenly matter.

A two-minute self-check before committing to FEIE

Before you mentally lock in FEIE for the year, it helps to ask a few blunt questions:

- Is most of my income *earned* compensation for services performed abroad, or is a meaningful portion investment or rental income?
- Is my host country's income tax rate on my wages low enough that credits won't fully offset U.S. tax?
- Do I expect major non-wage income that could be taxed at higher rates because of stacking?
- Am I self-employed, and if so, am I prepared for the possibility that self-employment tax may survive the exclusion?
- Is my compensation package simple enough that I can confidently source it to foreign workdays?

If those answers line up, FEIE can be the cleanest lever you have: a legitimate exclusion aimed directly at the paychecks that fund your day-to-day life overseas. If they don't line up, FEIE may still be part of the solution—but it shouldn't be the default setting.

3.2 Qualifying Through Bona Fide Residence or Physical Presence

FEIE eligibility has a "two locks, one keyring" feel. One lock is *tax home*—your main place of business has to be abroad, and the "abode" concept can still trip you up if your life is essentially anchored in the United States. The other lock is the one most people obsess over: you must qualify through either *bona fide residence* or *physical presence*. Two different paths, both legitimate, and they reward very different lifestyles.

The easiest way to choose between them is to ignore the names. "Bona fide residence" sounds like a visa category; "physical presence" sounds like a passport stamp contest. Neither label captures what the IRS is really testing. One path is about whether your overseas life is real and settled. The other is about whether the calendar proves you were out of the United States long enough—regardless of why, and regardless of what you meant to do.

Bona fide residence: the IRS asks whether you actually live there

Bona fide residence is the "whole life" test. It doesn't hinge on a single number of days; it hinges on whether your facts read like residence rather than a long business trip. Your housing, your routine, your job, your community ties, your intent—these are the kinds of clues that make the story believable.

The catch is baked into the definition: to use the bona fide residence test, you must be a bona fide resident of a foreign country (or countries) for an *uninterrupted period that includes an entire tax year*. That "entire tax year" requirement is what makes this test feel unfair to people who move mid-year. It's not judging how legitimate your move was; it's simply saying the timeline doesn't fit the rule yet.

That doesn't mean the year you move is a dead zone. It means bona fide residence may not be available for that year. Someone who starts living abroad in July 2025 may not meet the bona fide residence test for 2025 because it doesn't include an entire tax year. That person may still qualify under physical presence, or may use the filing timing approaches described in IRS materials (as we saw with extension and amended-return mechanics) if the facts later support an entire-year residence period.

Bona fide residence is also the more "human" test when your travel is messy. If your job requires frequent movement—regional management, offshore rotations, multi-country assignments—day counting can become a spreadsheet nightmare. Bona fide residence can be a better fit when the center of gravity is clearly outside the U.S., but your itinerary is too chaotic to cleanly engineer a 330-day window without sweating every layover.

What convinces the IRS you're genuinely resident

No single document confers bona fide residence the way a driver's license confers permission to drive. You build the case through consistent evidence. The strongest proof tends to be boring—and that's a compliment.

A long-term lease or home purchase abroad helps, but only if your pattern of life matches it. Local registration cards, residency permits, and work authorization can support the story, yet they don't automatically win it. The IRS is trying to decide whether you *moved your life* or simply *relocated your work.*

Think in terms of "receipts of normal life":

- a stable address and utility bills in your name,
- local bank activity that looks like everyday living (not just salary deposits and ATM withdrawals),
- local health coverage or doctor records,
- school records if you have children,
- membership in local professional organizations,
- a pattern of being abroad that doesn't look like constant commuting back to the U.S.

This kind of evidence does double duty. It supports bona fide residence, and it helps defend your *tax home* position if "abode" is a risk in your facts (for example, if your spouse and kids are still stateside, or you maintain a home you treat as the emotional headquarters of your life).

The price of the bona fide residence test: patience

Bona fide residence is a long-game test. It wants an uninterrupted period that includes an entire tax year. That's why people who expect to stay abroad for a long time often find it mentally soothing: once you're truly established, you're not living and dying by a day-count threshold every year.

But patience cuts both ways. If you're newly abroad and want the exclusion immediately, physical presence is often the faster route, because it can be satisfied by a 12-month period that straddles two tax years. Bona fide residence is less flexible on timing because of that "entire tax year" anchor.

So one way to summarize the choice is: bona fide residence rewards stability; physical presence rewards planning.

Physical presence: the calendar is the judge, and it doesn't care why

Physical presence is brutally simple. You must be physically present in one or more foreign countries for at least *330 full days during a 12-month period* that includes some part of the tax year. A "full day" is essentially midnight-to-midnight. Partial days don't count, which makes travel days sneakily expensive.

The rule's most surprising feature is also its best planning feature: the 12-month period can be *any consecutive 12-month window*. It does not have to match the calendar year. That flexibility creates legitimate planning opportunities—especially in the first year you go abroad—but it also creates misunderstandings when someone assumes "I was abroad most of the year" is good enough.

Physical presence has no sympathy clause. You either have 330 full days abroad or you don't. The reason for missing days doesn't matter. If you fail the day count, you fail the test—regardless of whether you came back for a family emergency, an illness, or because your employer ordered you home.

That harshness is precisely why physical presence is both popular and risky. It's popular because it feels objective. It's risky because objectivity can be unforgiving.

The hidden art of selecting your 12-month window

The 12-month window is the most powerful dial you can turn under the physical presence test. Get it right, and a mid-year mover can qualify surprisingly quickly. Get it wrong, and you can miss the 330-day threshold by a handful of days and lose the whole benefit.

A practical example: suppose you move abroad mid-year and want FEIE for that tax year. You may be able to choose a 12-month period that starts in the middle of the year and runs into the next year, reaching 330 full days abroad within that chosen window. Then, on Form 2555, you generally compute the exclusion based on the qualifying days that fall within the tax year (which effectively prorates the annual limit to the portion of the year you qualified).

This is where "any 12-month period" becomes more than trivia. It's the difference between "no exclusion until next year" and "partial exclusion now."

That flexibility also means you can accidentally choose a window that is *technically valid* but *strategically foolish*. Many taxpayers grab January 1 to December 31 because that's how humans think, and then wonder why they can't reach 330 days after moving in June. The calendar year is not the default under physical presence; it's just one of many possible windows.

The travel-day trap: how 36 days in the U.S. can blow it up

Because physical presence requires 330 full foreign days in a 12-month period, you can have no more than 35 days that are not full foreign days within that window. The moment you go beyond that, you're done.

A classic trap is a taxpayer who spends 36 days in the United States during the chosen 12-month period—perhaps a holiday visit plus a work trip plus a wedding—and ends up with fewer than 330 full foreign days. The exclusion is lost, even if the trip was compelled by illness or employer orders.

The emotional sting here is that the taxpayer may genuinely have "lived abroad" all year in the everyday sense. But physical presence is not evaluating your identity; it's evaluating your days.

If your schedule tends to include frequent U.S. visits, physical presence becomes a constraint you have to manage proactively. It's not enough to be generally overseas; you must protect the 330-day count like it's a fragile instrument.

Airport days, layovers, and the cost of being in transit

Physical presence turns travel days into puzzle pieces. The concept of a "full day" means the day you depart the U.S. and the day you arrive back in the U.S. are usually not full foreign days. Depending on the itinerary, you may lose additional days to time zones and stops.

This is where people get burned by assumptions like "I was only in the U.S. for two weeks." The IRS doesn't count "weeks." It counts midnights. If you leave the U.S. late on a Monday and arrive abroad Tuesday, you likely didn't get a full foreign day for Monday. If you return to the U.S. early on a Monday, you likely didn't get a full foreign day for Monday either. Those edge-days can add up.

The practical move is to keep a clean travel log and reconcile it to something objective (passport stamps, flight itineraries, calendar entries, location history). Under audit pressure, "I'm pretty sure" is a weak foundation for a benefits claim.

Bona fide residence vs. physical presence: personality fit

If bona fide residence and physical presence were job interviews, they'd ask different questions.

Bona fide residence asks: "Where do you belong day-to-day?" Physical presence asks: "Where were you at midnight?"

Some taxpayers naturally fit one test:

The planted expat. A long-term contract, an apartment lease that renews, kids in local school, weekends that look normal. Bona fide residence often matches this life cleanly.

The highly mobile professional. Rotations, regional travel, uncertain assignment length, but a calendar that can still be engineered to hit 330 full days abroad. Physical presence can work well if travel is tracked and the window is chosen strategically.

The U.S. tethered commuter. Lots of U.S. return trips, maybe a spouse or business still stateside, a home maintained "just in case." Both tests can be harder here: physical presence may fail on days, and bona fide residence may be harder to substantiate if the center of life still reads as American. This is where the tax home/abode issue (as we saw) tends to show up with teeth.

The digital nomad. Multiple countries, short stays, constant movement. Physical presence can work if the day count works, because it allows "one or more foreign countries." Bona fide residence can be difficult because it is about being a resident of *a* foreign country (or countries) in a bona fide sense, not perpetually in transit without establishing a stable life.

Digital nomads sometimes assume the physical presence test is automatically safe. It can be, but it pushes you into record-keeping mode. The IRS may not care that you felt "abroad" all year if your stamps, itineraries, and accommodation receipts don't line up neatly.

Split-year moves: the year you leave and the year you return

The two tests behave very differently during transition years.

When you *depart* the U.S. mid-year, physical presence is often the practical choice because you can use a 12-month window that starts after departure and reaches 330 days by stretching into the following year. Your FEIE amount for that first year generally reflects only the qualifying days that fall within that tax year.

Bona fide residence usually can't help in the departure year if you didn't reside abroad for an uninterrupted period that includes an entire tax year. The rule is simply built that way. Some taxpayers respond by waiting and claiming later once the "entire tax year" requirement is satisfied, using the filing timing approaches that IRS guidance permits. Others use physical presence for the first year and then consider bona fide residence afterward if their overseas life stabilizes.

When you *return* to the U.S. mid-year, physical presence may still work for the part of the year you were abroad, depending on the chosen 12-month window and your travel. Bona fide residence can also sometimes apply if your uninterrupted residence period included a full tax year before you returned. The details can be subtle, especially when you're trying to align the rule's "uninterrupted period" language with real life: moving apartments, changing jobs, relocating from one country to another.

The key takeaway is that move years are rarely "plug and play." They're the years when FEIE is most valuable—and also the years when the rules most often produce surprises.

Frequent U.S. travel: treat your day count like a budget

For physical presence, treat U.S. days the way you'd treat a spending budget with a hard cap. The 12-month window allows only 35 days that are not full foreign days if you want to reach 330 full days abroad. That's not much. A week for Thanksgiving, a week for a conference, a week for a family event, plus travel days—suddenly you're near the edge.

That budgeting mindset changes behavior. You stop scheduling "quick" U.S. trips in a way that burns extra edge-days. You stop assuming that a layover "doesn't count." You stop trusting memory and start tracking.

For bona fide residence, U.S. travel is less about a numeric cap and more about the narrative. Occasional visits are normal. Constant back-and-forth can make the overseas residence feel less bona fide. If your pattern resembles commuting, you're asking the IRS to bless a story your own boarding passes contradict.

What records actually matter (and why you want them before you need them)

FEIE disputes often boil down to a boring fight: not what you intended, but what you can prove.

For physical presence, records that anchor location by date are gold:

- flight itineraries and boarding passes,
- passport stamps (when available),
- entry/exit records from countries that provide them,
- contemporaneous calendars,
- employer travel logs,
- location history from a phone account (used carefully and consistently).

For bona fide residence, records that anchor *life* are persuasive:

- leases, renewal letters, and move-in/move-out documents,
- local registration and residency permits,
- local pay statements and employment contracts,
- evidence of community ties (schools, clubs, professional memberships),

- local medical or insurance records.

The common mistake is trying to build these retroactively. When a benefit is worth thousands of dollars, "I can probably find that email" is not a strategy. It's a hope.

A reality check about visas, leases, and "official" status

A visa can be strong supporting evidence. It is not a substitute for the test.

Some people assume a work visa or residency permit automatically means bona fide residence. Others assume that without a residency permit—say, because they're in a country on a status that feels temporary—they can't be bona fide residents. Real life is messier than that. Immigration status and tax residence are related, but they're not identical systems.

Similarly, a lease can be evidence of residence, but it can also be a prop. A rented apartment you never sleep in doesn't create bona fide residence. On the other hand, plenty of genuine residents live in employer-provided housing or short-term rentals because that's normal in their industry or city.

The useful mental model is: the IRS is not grading your paperwork; it is grading the coherence of your facts.

Choosing the test that gives you the least anxiety

Some expats prefer physical presence because it's measurable. They can count days, build a spreadsheet, and know where they stand. Others hate the brittleness—one extra U.S. trip and the whole claim collapses—so they prefer bona fide residence once they're settled.

There's also a temperament factor. If you're the kind of person who keeps receipts and tracks miles, physical presence is manageable. If you're the kind of person who can't remember what you ate yesterday, day counting can turn tax season into a detective novel you didn't want to write.

The best choice is the one you can defend calmly. FEIE is valuable, but it's not worth chronic stress. If you're constantly flirting with the 330-day edge, bona fide residence may be a better long-term fit if your facts support it. If you're new abroad and don't yet have a full tax year of residence, physical presence may be the bridge.

One last constraint that shapes everything: tax home and "abode"

It's tempting to treat the two tests as the whole game. They aren't. Eligibility requires meeting the tax home test (and avoiding disqualifying "abode" ties) plus either the bona fide residence test or the physical presence test.

That means you can have a perfect 330-day spreadsheet and still have trouble if your life is effectively centered in the United States. Or you can have a sincere intention to live overseas and still fail if your work situation doesn't support a foreign tax home. The two locks matter.

The practical takeaway is not paranoia; it's alignment. Your paperwork, your travel, your living arrangement, and your story should point in the same direction. When those elements line up, either test becomes far less mysterious—and far easier to defend if anyone asks you to prove it.

3.3 Defining Foreign Earned Income and Common Compensation Traps

"Foreign earned income" sounds like a geographic label you can slap onto a paycheck. In practice it behaves more like a spotlight: it illuminates *compensation for personal services performed* in a foreign country during the period you qualify, and it leaves everything else in the dark. The hard part isn't the concept—it's the modern paystub. Global compensation has become a junk drawer of items that don't politely announce what they are for U.S. purposes.

A useful mindset: the IRS isn't impressed by where the money *lands*. Paid in dollars? Irrelevant. Deposited into a U.S. bank? Still irrelevant. Employer headquartered in New York? Not the deciding factor. The IRS wants to know: *Where were you when you did the work that created this pay?* That single question settles most sourcing disputes—and creates most of the traps.

The sourcing rule that runs the show: where services are performed

For FEIE, sourcing is based on where services are performed. If you did the work in a foreign country, it generally points toward foreign-source compensation; if you did the work in the United States, it generally points toward U.S.-source compensation. Simple enough—until you add a laptop, a plane ticket, and a compensation package with a bonus, equity, and an allowance that your employer calls "non-taxable."

Mixed work locations are where people accidentally over-claim FEIE. It's common to hear, "I live overseas, so my salary is foreign." But if you spent meaningful time working physically in the U.S., part of that salary may be tied to U.S. workdays. The same is true for a bonus that rewards a year of performance spanning both places. FEIE doesn't magically bless all pay received while you hold an overseas address; it follows the labor.

This becomes especially important for anyone who does any of the following:

- flies to the U.S. for quarterly meetings or project sprints,
- works a hybrid arrangement where "home base" is abroad but the team is stateside,

- splits the year between two countries for personal reasons while keeping one job,
- supports multiple clients and occasionally performs services during U.S. visits.

The good news is that the logic is consistent. The bad news is that your calendar now matters as much as your W-2.

Mixed workdays: the allocation problem nobody budgets time for

Imagine you're employed by a company that pays you a steady salary all year. You spend most of the year abroad, but you make several U.S. work trips. From a payroll perspective, your pay is smooth and continuous. From a sourcing perspective, it's lumpy: some of your compensation is tied to foreign workdays, and some is tied to U.S. workdays.

In many real-life cases, a reasonable approach is to allocate wages based on workdays in each location (or another reasonable method consistent with the facts). That's not busywork; it's the difference between a defensible FEIE position and a hand-wave.

A common mistake is treating travel as "personal time" because the trip was short, or because you kept sleeping in your childhood bedroom and it didn't feel like "work." If you were physically in the U.S. and performing services, those are U.S. workdays. The IRS doesn't care that you were jet-lagged, working from a hotel, or eating takeout at 11 p.m. You were in the country, doing the job.

If you want one practical habit that pays for itself: keep a travel log that distinguishes *where you were* from *why you were there.* "Conference: Chicago" is not enough. You want dates, locations, and whether you worked those days. Later, when you're staring at a bonus that needs to be sourced, your own notes become the difference between clarity and guesswork.

Qualifying periods gate what you can exclude

FEIE is not only about *where* the work happened; it's also about *when* you qualified to claim the exclusion. Only earned income from foreign sources earned during qualifying periods is eligible for exclusion. That "during" matters more than people realize.

This gating effect shows up when:

- you move abroad mid-year,
- you return to the U.S. mid-year,
- you have a period of qualification under one test that starts or ends at a specific date,
- compensation is paid after the work is performed (bonuses, commissions, deferred payouts).

Many taxpayers intuitively treat the FEIE limit as a yearly coupon: qualify at some point, apply it to the year's wages, done. The actual mechanics are stricter. The exclusion amount is tied to the time you qualify within the year, and income must relate to services performed during qualifying periods. That's why those move-year returns can feel surprisingly technical, and why timing your start date, end date, and travel can have a real dollar impact.

Bonuses: one paycheck, two years, three problems

Bonuses are where the neat story breaks. A bonus is often paid in the following year, based on prior-year performance, and may be tied to a period during which you worked in multiple countries. That creates three separate questions:

1. *Timing:* What tax year is the bonus income included in (often the year you receive it, for cash-basis taxpayers)?
2. *Sourcing:* What portion of the bonus relates to services performed abroad versus in the U.S.?

3. *Qualifying period:* Did the services occur during your qualifying period for FEIE?

The trap is assuming a bonus is sourced based on where you were when it hit your bank account. That's emotionally satisfying—"I was abroad when it paid, so it's foreign"—and frequently wrong. If the bonus rewards a year of work, the sourcing tends to follow the work.

Another trap is forgetting that a bonus paid in January can be the largest "new" income item on that year's return. If you moved back to the U.S. in December, a January bonus may arrive after your qualifying period ends. The result can be counterintuitive: a payment connected to your overseas assignment becomes taxable in a year you no longer qualify. Form 2555 instructions contain rules for income received in a later year but earned in a prior year, and that's precisely the kind of rule that becomes relevant when bonus cycles collide with move dates.

If your compensation includes large bonuses, it's worth coordinating HR/payroll details with your tax planning. Bonus design—performance year, payout date, whether it's discretionary or formula-based—can change how easy it is to support a sourcing allocation.

Allowances, reimbursements, and "tax-free" employer language

Expat packages love allowances: housing, cost of living, education, transportation, home leave, per diems, "mobility premiums." Locally, some of these may be treated as non-taxable or taxed favorably. Your employer might also describe them as "tax-free" in offer letters, which is a phrase that should make a U.S. taxpayer immediately suspicious.

For U.S. purposes, many allowances and employer-paid benefits are still compensation. Some may qualify as foreign earned income; some may not; some may be excluded under other rules;

some may be taxable but eligible for FEIE if they otherwise meet the requirements. The point isn't to memorize which bucket each allowance goes into—the point is to recognize that "allowance" is not a tax category. It's a label your employer uses.

A useful test: ask what the payment is *for*.

- If it's paying you for being willing to work somewhere (a premium), it often behaves like compensation.
- If it's reimbursing you for a business expense under an accountable arrangement, it may not be taxable compensation at all.
- If it's paying a personal expense without requiring substantiation, it tends to drift back toward taxable wages.

The documentation rule of life: reimbursements that are supported by receipts and returned excess amounts are easier to defend as reimbursements. Flat payments with no substantiation tend to behave like additional pay. When expats get tripped up, it's often because they treated a flat "living allowance" as somehow outside the tax system, when it was effectively salary in a different costume.

Employer-provided housing and other noncash benefits

Noncash benefits can feel "invisible" because they don't show up as cash in your bank account. But if they appear on a pay statement, a year-end tax form, or an internal benefits summary, they may be part of your compensation for U.S. purposes.

Housing is the classic example. If your employer pays your landlord directly, it can still be taxable compensation depending on the details. If your employer provides a company apartment, the value may be treated as a benefit. Whether and how those items interact with FEIE and the separate housing benefit is where planning becomes very specific to facts.

The trap here is psychological: expats often treat anything paid directly by the employer as "not income" because it doesn't pass through their hands. The IRS does not share that intuition. The tax system is perfectly happy to treat value you received as income, whether you touched cash or not.

U.S. government pay abroad: the exception people learn too late

One of the most important "don't assume" rules: U.S. government pay as an employee does not qualify for FEIE or housing benefits.

This is the kind of rule that feels personal because it's blunt. If you're a civilian employee of the U.S. government posted abroad, or military personnel, you may feel like the poster child for overseas work. But FEIE simply does not apply to that category of pay.

Why does this matter beyond the individuals directly affected? Because it illustrates a broader lesson: FEIE eligibility isn't based on your mailing address or the fact that your job is overseas. It's based on statutory conditions that can carve out exceptions that surprise reasonable people. If your employer is a government entity—or if you work under a contract structure that resembles government employment—this is a "verify early" issue, not a "discover at filing time" issue.

Self-employment: same sourcing idea, more places to stumble

For self-employed expats—consultants, freelancers, online service providers—the sourcing rule is conceptually the same: where were you when you performed the services?

In practice, self-employment creates two extra wrinkles.

First, it's easier to blur work and life. If you answer client emails on a U.S. visit, that's still performing services. If you travel to the U.S. for a conference and do client work from the hotel at night, those are U.S. workdays. It's not the glamour trip that counts; it's the physical location during service performance.

Second, your records are your responsibility. Employees often have corporate travel logs, HR records, and payroll statements that unintentionally help them. Self-employed people have invoices and payment processors, which rarely say "services performed in Country X." If you ever need to defend sourcing, you want contracts, project timelines, calendars, and a credible story for where you did the work.

Self-employment also tends to introduce business structures—partnerships, corporations—that can change how income is characterized and sourced. The IRS explicitly flags special compensation categories needing careful handling, including partnership/-corporate income structures, and directs readers to Publication 54 for detailed treatment. Translation: if you operate through an entity, don't assume the FEIE analysis is identical to a simple sole proprietor who works from a kitchen table abroad.

Equity compensation: the pay that refuses to sit still

If salary is a straight line, equity pay is a web.

Stock options, restricted stock units (RSUs), employee stock purchase plans, and other equity awards often vest over time. That "over time" is the problem. A grant might be made while you're in the U.S., vest while you're abroad, and be sold after you return. Meanwhile, the compensation element may be tied to a service period that spans multiple locations.

The IRS explicitly flags stock options as requiring careful handling for a reason. Equity compensation is one of the fastest ways to turn a seemingly simple FEIE return into a sourcing and allocation project.

The most common trap isn't technical; it's emotional. Equity pay often arrives as a pleasant surprise—"I forgot those RSUs vest this month"—and surprises are exactly what tax planning hates. If you have equity compensation:

- know your vesting calendar,
- know what events create taxable income for U.S. purposes (grant, vest, exercise, sale—depending on the type),
- expect that an allocation may be needed if your service period spans both U.S. and foreign workdays.

Equity pay also tends to collide with payroll mechanics. Some companies run equity through a home-country payroll system regardless of where you are physically based, or they "gross up" taxes in one jurisdiction. Those payroll decisions don't determine FEIE eligibility by themselves, but they do affect what gets reported, when, and how messy reconciliation becomes.

Payroll split arrangements: one job, two pay statements, and a filing headache

Global employers sometimes split payroll: part of your compensation runs through a U.S. payroll and part through a local payroll, or one entity pays your base and another pays allowances. This can happen for compliance reasons, benefits administration, or sheer corporate inertia.

The trap is assuming that "U.S. payroll" means "U.S.-source" and "local payroll" means "foreign-source." Payroll location is an administrative choice. Sourcing is about where you perform the services. A U.S. payroll can pay compensation for work done abroad; a local payroll can pay compensation for work done in the U.S. (for example, a business trip). You still need to line up the pay with the place the work happened.

Payroll splits can also create duplicate reporting, mismatched totals, and confusion over which items are wages versus reimbursements. If you receive two year-end wage statements (or a wage statement plus an equivalent local form), reconciliation becomes part of your tax life. A good habit is to maintain a "shadow paystub" spreadsheet: total compensation by type (salary, bonus, allowance, equity) and by time period, mapped to where you were working. It's not glamorous, but it saves you from relying on intuition.

The "I was abroad, so it must be excludable" fallacy

A lot of FEIE mistakes come from treating physical location as a magic stamp on income. But different income categories follow different rules.

Unearned income items (dividends/interest/capital gains and retirement-type payments) do not qualify as foreign earned income even if received while you are overseas. That can feel unfair: you're abroad, you pay local tax, your U.S. broker sends a statement, and the IRS still calls it non-qualifying for FEIE. But FEIE's domain is compensation for services. Passive income is a different system.

The practical consequence is that many expats end up with a "split return": part of the return is about excluding qualifying compensation, and part of it is about everything else—often taxed at rates influenced by stacking, and often eligible for relief through other mechanisms rather than FEIE. That's why simply maxing the FEIE isn't always the best overall outcome.

A quick diagnostic: which compensation items deserve a second look

When you're deciding what qualifies for FEIE, a few items are routinely worth extra scrutiny because they're so often mischaracterized:

- *Bonuses and commissions* (timing and multi-country service periods)
- *Allowances* (taxable compensation vs. true reimbursements)
- *Noncash benefits* (housing, vehicles, education support)

- *Equity compensation* (vesting/exercise/sale and allocations)
- *Pay received after you move* (especially after returning to the U.S.)
- *Any pay tied to U.S. work trips* (sourcing by service location)

None of these are reasons to panic. They're reasons to slow down. FEIE rewards confidence backed by records, not confidence backed by vibes.

The practical takeaway: treat your compensation like a story that must be consistent

A defensible FEIE position is basically a coherent story told in numbers:

- You qualified for FEIE during a specific period.
- During that period, you performed services in foreign countries on specific days.
- You received compensation for those services.
- The amount you exclude tracks the portion of compensation connected to those services and that period.

When the story is consistent, FEIE feels clean. When the story has contradictions—bonus paid after the move, equity vesting across borders, "tax-free" allowances that are really just extra pay—FEIE can still work, but it becomes a careful sourcing and documentation project.

And that's the real dividing line between easy FEIE and stressful FEIE: not whether you're abroad, but whether your compensation package behaves like a simple salary or like a multi-country jigsaw puzzle.

3.4 Adding the Foreign Housing Exclusion or Deduction

Rent is the expense that makes expatriate life feel most real. You can ignore currency swings for a while. You can pretend the grocery bill is "roughly the same." You cannot pretend your apartment in Zurich costs what your apartment in Phoenix cost. That sticker shock is exactly why the foreign housing benefit exists: it's the FEIE's practical sidekick, designed to give extra relief when your overseas housing costs are legitimately high.

The housing benefit is not a free-for-all deduction for "anything with a roof." It's a separate lever from FEIE and is computed as housing expenses minus a base housing amount; that base housing amount is tied to the FEIE maximum. In other words, the IRS isn't trying to subsidize ordinary housing costs. It's trying to recognize the *extra* cost of maintaining a home abroad—especially in expensive markets—above a built-in floor.

Exclusion vs. deduction: same idea, different label

The benefit comes in two flavors depending on how you earn your money:

- *Foreign housing exclusion* for employees.
- *Foreign housing deduction* for self-employed individuals.

Mechanically, both start with the same core computation (eligible housing expenses minus the base amount). The difference is where the benefit shows up on your return and what it offsets. The employee version is framed as an exclusion—conceptually, part of your compensation is treated as non-taxable. The self-employed version is framed as a deduction—conceptually, it reduces income.

The takeaway isn't "memorize which one you are." It's: don't miss the benefit because you assumed "housing exclusion" is only for employees, or because you assumed self-employment means you're out of luck. The benefit exists in both forms; it just wears different clothing.

The base housing amount: why modest rent often produces no housing benefit

The base housing amount is the single feature that confuses people the most because it feels like the IRS moving the goalposts. You track your rent, utilities, and qualifying expenses, do the math, and then discover the first chunk doesn't count.

That's not a bug; it's the design. The housing benefit is meant to cover *excess* housing costs. If your eligible expenses don't rise above the base, there may be little or no additional benefit to claim.

The numbers matter here, so it helps to see one concrete set of amounts. For 2026, the base housing amount for a full-year qualified individual is \$21,264 ($16\% \times \$132,900$). Read that as the "floor" for the year: the IRS treats roughly that level of housing cost as normal enough that it doesn't create extra relief.

Now imagine you have \$25,000 of eligible housing expenses for the year. The amount potentially available for the housing exclusion/deduction is not \$25,000. It's \$25,000 minus the base housing amount. That means only \$3,736 is in play. People in moderately priced cities sometimes do all the tracking, all the receipt saving, all the effort—and end up with a benefit that feels comically small. That result doesn't mean they did something wrong. It means their housing costs weren't far above the built-in threshold.

The flip side is what makes the housing benefit feel magical in expensive places: once your costs climb far above the base, the benefit becomes meaningful fast.

The other limit: you can't exclude unlimited housing costs

There's a second governor on the system: a cap on how much housing expense can be counted in the first place. For 2026, the general max housing expenses for a full year are $39,870 ($30\% \times \$132,900$), unless a higher locality limit applies.

That general cap is a critical reality check. If your rent plus utilities plus other eligible costs exceed that amount, you don't automatically get to use the entire total. The system is designed to provide relief, but within a bounded range.

This is where people in extreme cost markets can feel whiplash. Your rent may be high enough to make you laugh at the idea of a "cap," and yet the tax computation insists one exists. Which brings us to the most important exception.

High-cost localities: the IRS admits some cities are just brutal

The standard cap isn't the last word for everyone. High-cost localities have higher limits, and the IRS publishes annual adjusted limitations by city/country. Those lists are updated each year in the Internal Revenue Bulletin.

This is the part of the housing benefit that feels almost like a secret menu: two taxpayers with identical rent can get different results depending on where they live. One in a non-listed city is capped at the general limit. Another in a listed high-cost city may use a higher locality cap that better reflects local reality.

A quick example makes it tangible. Picture two employees with the same salary and the same $4,000/month rent (plus similar utilities). One lives in a city that isn't on the high-cost list; the eligible expense cap can pinch. The other lives in a city that *is* on the list; the higher cap means more of those real costs can be counted. Same rent. Same year. Different tax outcome—purely because the IRS agrees one market is officially more expensive.

For planners, the annual nature of these lists matters. A city can move on or off the high-cost table, and the limits can change. If you're committing to a lease in a pricey location, the housing cap is not a set-it-and-forget-it number.

A planning wrinkle: you may be able to use next year's higher limit

In a rare move that rewards attentive taxpayers, IRB 2026-17 provides an option allowing certain taxpayers to apply the 2026 adjusted housing limits to the 2025 taxable year if the 2026 limit is higher for their locality.

That's not an everyday tactic, but it's a powerful concept: housing limits are not static, and IRS guidance can sometimes allow a later, higher limit to be applied to an earlier year. This is especially relevant if you're amending a return or finalizing a year where you lived in a high-cost locality and the updated tables materially improve your cap.

If you've ever wondered why experienced expat preparers seem to watch Internal Revenue Bulletin updates like sports scores, this is why. The housing benefit is one of the few places where a published table can swing the result.

What counts as housing expenses: think "keeping a home," not "building wealth"

The phrase "housing expenses" invites creativity. The IRS responds by drawing boundaries: certain expenses count because they're part of maintaining a place to live, and certain expenses do not because they're essentially buying an asset or improving one.

Form 2555 instructions specify disallowed housing expense items. The big ones that tempt people are:

- costs of buying or improving a house,

- mortgage principal,
- depreciation,
- and other specified exclusions in the instructions.

Those disallowed items reveal the philosophy: the housing benefit is not intended to subsidize home ownership or renovations. It's aimed at the cost of *having* housing, not the cost of *investing* in housing.

That distinction can feel unfair if you're in a market where renting is impractical and buying is the norm. But the rule is what it is. Trying to force mortgage principal or improvements into the computation is one of the cleanest ways to create a problem on a return that otherwise would have been easy.

The "reasonable and ordinary" problem: reality beats categories

Even among expenses that *sound* like housing, the facts matter. Some arrangements are straightforward: rent paid monthly, utilities billed separately, a security deposit, maybe renters' insurance. Others are messy: serviced apartments, employer-paid leases, bundled payments that combine rent and cleaning and internet and parking in one line item.

The practical task is to separate the housing element from the lifestyle element. If your lease includes a housekeeping service, the IRS isn't automatically agreeing that a weekly deep clean is a housing necessity. If the landlord charges you an "amenity fee" for a gym and concierge, that's not necessarily housing expense in the sense the rules intend. If the only way to rent in your city is through a serviced apartment model, you may still have a defensible position—but you want to document what the payment covers.

A safe instinct is to treat anything that resembles luxury add-ons as suspicious. Not because you're doing something immoral by paying for comfort, but because the tax rules are not written to subsidize comfort. They're written to recognize unavoidable cost differences.

Employer-provided housing: don't assume you can't claim anything

Employer involvement often makes taxpayers throw up their hands. "The company paid the landlord directly, so I guess I'm not paying housing expenses." That can be wrong. Employer-provided arrangements can still interact with the housing benefit, but they tend to demand careful reading of what's being provided and how it's treated in your compensation.

If employer-paid housing is included in your taxable compensation for U.S. purposes, it may effectively be part of the pool of compensation you're trying to shelter using FEIE and the housing exclusion. If the employer arrangement is structured differently, the analysis changes. The common thread is that you cannot decide purely based on cash flow. You decide based on the tax characterization of the benefit.

This is one of those areas where your paystub details matter more than your bank account. If the housing value appears as taxable wages or a reportable benefit, it's waving a flag that it belongs in the conversation.

Documentation: the housing benefit rewards receipts like a loyalty program

The housing benefit is unusually documentation-driven because it's built from actual expenses. That means you want:

- a signed lease (and renewals),
- proof of payment (bank transfers, receipts, landlord statements),

- utility bills (or a clear breakdown if utilities are bundled),
- a way to translate local currency amounts consistently for U.S. reporting,
- records that tie the expenses to the period you qualified.

Notice that last point: timing matters. The housing benefit is tied to qualifying periods just like the income exclusion is. If you qualify for only part of the year, the limits and base amounts are effectively prorated. The more your year resembles a move, the more important it is that expenses line up with the months you actually qualified.

A practical habit that reduces pain: create a single "housing folder" (digital or physical) the moment you sign a lease abroad. Drop every housing-related record into it as it arrives. Trying to reconstruct utilities from old emails in March is the tax equivalent of trying to reassemble a shredded document.

How housing relief changes the FEIE decision

The housing benefit can change the economics of claiming FEIE because it can extend the relief beyond the base FEIE limit—particularly for employees in high-cost cities. Someone whose salary exceeds the FEIE cap may still be able to exclude additional amounts through the housing exclusion, depending on expenses and caps.

It can also change behavior in subtler ways. Expats sometimes choose "company housing" or "housing allowance" structures without realizing the U.S. tax consequences differ dramatically depending on how the benefit is reported and whether it becomes taxable compensation. The same apartment can produce different U.S. results depending on whether it's framed as a reimbursement, an allowance, or a direct employer-provided benefit.

So the housing benefit becomes a planning lens: not only "what can I claim?" but "how should I structure housing support in the first place?" If you have negotiating leverage in an expat package, it can be worth thinking about how the benefit will be treated for U.S. purposes before you sign the offer letter.

The most common over-claim: treating ownership costs as housing expenses

The fastest way to turn a legitimate housing benefit into a red flag is to get creative with home ownership costs. A taxpayer buys a condo abroad and tries to feed the mortgage payment into the housing computation as if it were rent. Form 2555 instructions explicitly disallow mortgage principal and costs of buying or improving a house, and depreciation is also out.

That doesn't mean homeowners can never benefit. It means the housing benefit isn't designed to replicate the full cost of owning property. If you own abroad, you need to be especially careful to separate potentially eligible items from clearly disallowed ones, and to resist the very human urge to say, "But my mortgage is my housing cost." It is. It just isn't the kind of cost the housing benefit is trying to subsidize.

The most common under-claim: not tracking because you assume you'll hit the cap anyway

There's an opposite error that's quieter: not tracking expenses because you assume you'll max out the limit. High-cost city residents sometimes treat the housing calculation as pointless because "rent alone exceeds any cap." But the locality cap might be higher than you expect, and eligible expenses may include more than rent. The only way to know is to run the numbers with real documentation.

Also, caps and base amounts can change. A year that doesn't produce a benefit might become a year that does after an IRS locality table update or a change in your living arrangement. The housing benefit rewards attention—not because the IRS wants busywork, but because the rules are literally built from your real costs.

A grounded way to think about it

A simple mental model keeps you out of trouble: the housing benefit is a filter.

First filter: did you pay (or receive, as compensation) eligible housing expenses during a qualifying period? If no, stop.

Second filter: do your eligible expenses rise above the base housing amount? If no, the benefit may be minimal.

Third filter: are your expenses below the cap that applies to your location (general or high-cost locality)? If no, you may be limited.

Run those filters honestly, and the benefit is straightforward. Most problems come from skipping a filter: claiming expenses that are disallowed, ignoring the base amount, or forgetting that locality caps exist.

At its best, the housing exclusion or deduction does something rare in tax: it acknowledges a very real pain point of global work. It won't make a Hong Kong lease feel cheap. But it can make it feel less like you're paying a "rent premium" twice—once to your landlord and once to the IRS.

3.5 Election, Revocation, and Long-Term FEIE Planning

FEIE is less like a coupon and more like a setting on a machine. Once you flip the setting on, the machine keeps running that way until you deliberately change it—and the "change" lever has a guardrail that surprises people. This is why FEIE works best as a multi-year decision rather than a yearly reflex. The first year you qualify, claiming FEIE may feel like the obvious move. Five years later, you may discover that "obvious" came with strings.

The mechanics start simple: elections to receive FEIE and/or housing benefits are made via Form 2555. Regulations emphasize that elections are procedural, filed with an original or amended return, and the housing election is separate from the FEIE election. That last clause is not trivia. It means you can be an FEIE claimant who forgets to elect housing, or a housing claimant who doesn't claim the main exclusion, or someone who changes one election while leaving the other intact. The tax law treats them as related benefits, but it doesn't treat them as a single inseparable choice.

Form 2555: the election is made by doing, not by wishing

Many tax benefits are claimed by checking a box. FEIE isn't really that kind of benefit. You "choose" it by filling out the form that computes it and attaching it to the return. That may sound obvious, but it explains a common real-life mishap: a taxpayer qualifies, files a return without Form 2555, and only later realizes they left a large benefit on the table.

When that happens, the instinct is to ask whether the IRS will let you "retroactively choose FEIE." Sometimes the answer is yes, but the pathway matters. IRS guidance provides limited routes for late-filed elections (for example, within 1 year of the original due date), and in other situations the fix can require a private letter ruling and so-called 9100 relief—an administrative process that can be expensive and slow.

In plain language: if you qualified and forgot to claim, don't assume it's hopeless, and don't assume it's easy. The clock matters. Your filing posture matters. And the longer you wait, the more you turn an ordinary return into a procedural problem.

If you're self-filing, build a simple habit: if you think you qualify, confirm that Form 2555 is actually included in the final e-file package. If you use a preparer, ask to see the form. FEIE is too valuable to leave to assumption.

The housing election is separate (and that's a planning opportunity)

The housing benefit has its own election. You can elect FEIE without electing the housing exclusion/deduction, and vice versa. That separation can feel bureaucratic, but it has a practical upside: it lets you tailor the claim to your situation.

One year, your rent spikes because you relocate to a high-cost city or your employer stops subsidizing housing. Another year, you move to a cheaper market or live with family temporarily. Having separate elections means you're not forced into an all-or-nothing stance. You can claim FEIE alone, FEIE plus housing, or housing relief where it makes sense, as long as the eligibility and computation rules support it.

It also matters for couples. Elections are personal in the sense that each spouse's situation can differ—one may have wages, the other self-employment income; one may have qualifying housing expenses, the other may not; one may qualify under a clean physical presence schedule, the other has messy U.S. travel. Coordinating those facts can make the difference between a return that merely files and a return that actually optimizes.

The "sticky" part: FEIE persists unless you revoke it

Once chosen, the exclusion election remains in effect for that year and all later years unless revoked. This is where FEIE starts to behave like a long-term setting, not a yearly choice.

That persistence can be helpful. If you're in a stable situation—same country, same job, same pattern of travel—FEIE can become routine. You keep qualifying, you keep electing, and your U.S. income tax stays low or zero. The benefit becomes part of your financial baseline.

But persistence also means FEIE can become the default on your return long after it stops being the best move. People change countries. Income rises. Bonuses become meaningful. Investment accounts grow. A spouse begins working. A local tax regime changes. An expat package ends. Those life changes can flip the math from "exclude" to "credit" without any drama—except FEIE may still be sitting there in the return because it's what you've always done.

That's why it's worth consciously re-evaluating FEIE at life transition points rather than letting inertia drive.

Revocation: the five-year lockout that turns a small decision into a big one

Revoking FEIE isn't just "not claiming it this year." Revocation is a deliberate act, and it comes with a meaningful consequence: after revoking an election, a taxpayer generally can't claim the exclusion(s) again for the next 5 tax years without IRS approval.

This rule exists to prevent gaming—switching in and out of FEIE every year to cherry-pick whatever produces the lowest bill. But for normal humans with normal careers, it can still be a trap.

Here's the classic scenario. Early in your overseas career, you work in a low-tax jurisdiction, so FEIE is perfect. Later you move to a high-tax jurisdiction, where credits may be more efficient and FEIE can reduce the usefulness of those credits on the same income. So you revoke FEIE to use credits.

Then, two years later, your company transfers you back to a low-tax place, or your income drops, or your life changes in a way that makes FEIE attractive again. Now the five-year lockout matters. You may be stuck—unless you obtain IRS approval to re-elect.

The practical lesson: don't revoke casually. Treat revocation like a strategic commitment, not a housekeeping tweak.

Why people revoke FEIE in the first place

Revocation usually happens for one of a few reasons, and each one is tied to a shift in the underlying math:

You move from a low-tax to a high-tax country.

In a high-tax environment, credits can often offset U.S. liability efficiently. FEIE can reduce the pool of income that would otherwise support credit usage because FEIE can reduce FTC usability for taxes tied to excluded income. That makes FEIE less obviously beneficial—and sometimes clearly inferior.

Your income rises well above the FEIE limit.

When you far exceed the exclusion limit, FEIE becomes a partial shield. Credits may become more valuable because they can apply across the full income range, depending on your situation. FEIE may still help, but it's no longer the dominant factor.

You have significant non-wage income, and stacking effects bite.

As discussed earlier, FEIE's stacking calculation can leave your remaining taxable income exposed to higher rates. In some cases, leaving income taxable and offsetting with credits produces a better overall result.

You're optimizing for future years, not just the current year.

Because FEIE is persistent unless revoked, you might revoke to reposition your strategy for a multi-year plan. That's the right instinct. The wrong execution is revoking without considering the five-year rule.

Late elections: when "I forgot" becomes a procedural puzzle

Late elections are where smart expats get humbled. You can do everything else correctly—qualify, track days, maintain a tax home abroad—and still miss the benefit because the election wasn't properly made.

The IRS provides limited routes for late-filed elections, such as filing within 1 year of the original due date in certain circumstances. Outside those routes, you may need to ask for relief through private letter ruling procedures under the 9100 relief framework. That's not just paperwork; it's a process.

A practical takeaway: if you qualify in a year with major dollars at stake (big income, big housing expenses), it's worth double-checking the election mechanics before the filing deadline passes. FEIE is a benefit you can lose to process, not just to substance.

Long-term FEIE planning: think in "chapters" of your expat life

The most effective way to plan with FEIE is to stop thinking year-by-year and start thinking in multi-year phases. Most expat careers naturally fall into phases anyway:

Phase: the initial assignment.

You're new abroad, income may be moderate, travel back to the U.S. may be frequent (weddings, goodbyes, logistics), and housing costs may be unusually high because you haven't optimized yet. FEIE can be attractive, but the qualification mechanics and timing of moves can make the first year complicated.

Phase: stable residence.

You're settled, travel patterns normalize, housing becomes predictable, and your documentation improves. FEIE becomes easier to administer. This is the period where FEIE can quietly save significant U.S. tax with minimal friction—especially in lower-tax jurisdictions.

Phase: rising income and complex pay.

Promotions, bonuses, equity compensation, and side income appear. Now the FEIE limit becomes relevant, and the interaction with credit planning becomes more meaningful. This is often where the "exclude vs credit" question deserves a fresh look.

Phase: relocation or repatriation.

Moves change everything: qualifying periods, day counting, source allocation, bonus timing, and sometimes the entire local tax framework. The temptation is to make a quick switch to whatever seems best in the move year. That's exactly when the five-year revocation rule demands caution.

This "phase" model isn't a formula. It's a way to remember that FEIE isn't just a number on a form; it's a strategy that should track the reality of your life.

A practical decision lens: will you want FEIE again soon?

Before revoking FEIE, ask a question that sounds simple but has teeth: *How confident am I that FEIE won't be useful again for the next five tax years?*

If your career path suggests you may bounce between tax regimes—say, a company that frequently assigns people to the Middle East, then Europe, then Asia—you should be extremely careful. A decision that improves this year's return can reduce options later.

If your future is stable in a consistently high-tax country, revocation may be a clean strategic move. If your future is uncertain, you may prefer to keep FEIE in place or explore ways to coordinate FEIE and credit planning without triggering a revocation that locks you out.

"Not claiming" vs "revoking": don't assume they're the same

Many taxpayers mentally treat these as identical: "I just won't file Form 2555 this year." That can be a dangerous assumption.

Revocation has consequences. The five-year lockout is tied to revocation, not merely to your feelings about the benefit. The procedural rules around elections and revocations matter. If you're considering a switch, it's worth treating it as a formal planning decision and confirming how your approach will be characterized under the procedural rules. A casual omission can create an unintended outcome—either failing to revoke when you meant to, or triggering revocation consequences when you didn't.

If you work with a preparer, use direct language: "I want to revoke the FEIE election," or "I do not want to revoke; I want to evaluate." Ambiguity is the enemy here.

Coordinating FEIE with credit planning: the "don't waste your ammo" rule

The most valuable mindset in multi-year planning is resource allocation. FEIE is one resource: it removes qualifying compensation from U.S. taxation up to a limit. Credits are another resource: they can offset U.S. tax on certain income categories, but their usefulness depends on how much U.S. taxable income remains and how your income is categorized.

Because FEIE can reduce FTC usability for taxes tied to excluded income, you don't want to blindly exclude income that would have been more efficiently neutralized by credits—particularly in high-tax situations. On the other hand, you don't want to "save" FEIE out of habit and end up with U.S. tax in a low-tax jurisdiction just because you were trying to preserve credit capacity you don't have.

The best multi-year plans treat FEIE and credits as complementary tools, used in proportion to the reality of each year and the likely arc of the next few years.

The quiet power move: revisit FEIE at inflection points

You don't need to run a deep optimization model annually. But you do want to revisit the decision at moments that change the shape of your return:

- changing countries,
- crossing the FEIE limit by a wide margin,
- receiving significant equity compensation,
- shifting from employee to self-employed (or vice versa),
- moving into or out of a high-cost housing market,
- major changes in family income (a spouse begins working or stops working).

These are the moments when FEIE can shift from hero to side character—or from side character to hero—without warning.

FEIE is at its best when it's chosen deliberately, maintained intentionally, and revoked only when the next five years of your life make that decision feel calm rather than risky. That's the difference between using FEIE as a one-year trick and using it as a long-term strategy.

Chapter 4

Foreign Tax Credits, Treaties, and Other Double-Tax Relief

Many expats assume double taxation is solved by one magic rule. It is not. Sometimes the best move is the Foreign Earned Income Exclusion, but just as often the smarter answer is a credit, a treaty position, or a social-tax agreement hiding in plain sight. This chapter helps readers compare those tools like a strategist, not a guesser.

4.1 The Foreign Tax Credit in Plain English

Picture your tax life as two cashiers who don't talk to each other. One cashier lives where you actually live and work. The other is the IRS. Each one scans the same paycheck and says, "That'll be $X, please." The Foreign Tax Credit (FTC) is the rule that forces the IRS cashier to accept that you already paid the other cashier *real money*—and to subtract much of that payment from your U.S. income tax bill.

That's the core mental model: the U.S. still runs the math on your return, but then gives you a credit for certain income taxes you paid to another country (or a U.S. possession) on the same income. A credit reduces your U.S. tax *dollar for dollar*. If your credit is $1,000, your U.S. bill drops by $1,000. Not a percentage. Not "maybe." It's the closest thing the tax code offers to showing a receipt and saying, "I already paid."

The FTC is also psychologically clarifying, because it frames the real question expats face: *Is the place where I live already taking enough income tax that the IRS mostly steps aside?* In many high-tax countries, the honest answer is yes—at least for wages and salary. In low-tax countries, the answer is often no, and the FTC becomes more like a partial coupon than a full shield.

Credit versus deduction: the gift card versus the coupon

A tax *deduction* is like getting permission to buy less stuff. It reduces the amount of income that gets taxed. A tax *credit* is like a gift card handed to the cashier at the very end—after everything is rung up.

Here's why that matters in plain numbers.

Suppose your U.S. taxable income leads to a $10,000 U.S. income tax bill. Now suppose you paid $10,000 of qualifying income tax to the country where you live.

- With a *credit*, that $10,000 can generally reduce your $10,000 U.S. bill down toward $0 (subject to limits we'll get to later in this chapter).
- With a *deduction*, you don't subtract $10,000 from the bill. You subtract it from your *income*. If your marginal tax rate is, say, 24%, a $10,000 deduction might save roughly $2,400 of tax—not $10,000.

That gap is why seasoned expats perk up at the word *credit*. A deduction is valuable, but it's the "percentage off" sticker. A credit is the "pay with this" card.

There's also a behavioral trap here: it's common to hear someone say, "I deducted my taxes paid overseas." That's usually the weaker option for expats, and for many people the IRS expects you to use the credit method if you want meaningful relief. The credit is designed for this exact scenario: one income stream, two income tax systems, and a strong desire to avoid paying twice for the same year of your life.

What kinds of overseas taxes count (and what doesn't)

The FTC is picky about what it will recognize. It's not a general credit for "money I had to pay abroad." It's specifically aimed at *income taxes* (or taxes that function like an income tax). In every-day terms: the tax should be calculated based on income, profits, or net gain—not simply on ownership, spending, or payroll in the broad sense.

Common payments that often fit the FTC's comfort zone:

- A national income tax on wages, salary, bonuses, or self-employment profit.
- Subnational income taxes (think province, state, city) *if* they operate like an income tax and are imposed by a foreign country's jurisdiction.

Common payments people hope will count but often don't:

- Social insurance or payroll-style contributions that are more like Social Security than income tax (those fall into a different conversation—sometimes a very expensive one).
- Value-added taxes (VAT/GST) and sales taxes. Painful, yes. Income tax, no.
- Property taxes and wealth taxes (sometimes there are edge cases, but don't assume).

A practical way to sanity-check yourself: if the amount you pay changes mainly because your *income* changed—and the return looks like an income tax return—the FTC is probably relevant. If the payment exists because you bought something, owned something, or simply participated in a labor system, it may not be.

The FTC is not a "refund program"

One misconception causes more confusion than almost anything else: thinking of the FTC as free money. It isn't. It's a relief valve that tries to stop double taxation, not a rewards program for paying high tax elsewhere.

So what does that mean in real life?

If your U.S. income tax bill on your foreign-source income would have been $8,000, and you paid $12,000 of qualifying income tax to your country of residence, the IRS doesn't mail you a $4,000 thank-you check for being overtaxed abroad. The FTC can generally reduce your U.S. income tax on that income to zero, and the extra $4,000 becomes *excess credit*—something that may be usable in other years (carryover rules) but not a prize.

That framing matters because it helps you stop chasing the wrong strategy. Paying more tax abroad than you "need" to doesn't create a net win. It may create FTC capacity for later, but it's still cash out the door.

Why expats in high-tax countries often lean on the FTC

Once you live in a country with substantial income tax rates, the FTC starts to feel like gravity: unglamorous, inevitable, and quietly shaping everything. Here's why.

First, the FTC often lines up naturally with how your pay is already taxed. If you're employed abroad, tax is frequently withheld from each paycheck. By the time you think about your U.S. return, the foreign income tax has already been paid (or at least withheld), and the FTC becomes the mechanism that tells the IRS: "This income has already been taxed at the source of your day-to-day life."

Second, for many households in higher-tax jurisdictions, the foreign income tax bill can be large enough that the FTC wipes out most or all U.S. income tax on the same income. That's the dream scenario for double-tax relief: you still file, but you don't relive the pain twice.

Third—and this is where planning gets interesting—the FTC can preserve parts of your U.S. return that exclusions can shrink. The FEIE can be powerful, but it removes income from your U.S. tax base, and that can have side effects (especially around credits and calculations that depend on taxable income). The FTC, by contrast, keeps the income in the computation and then offsets the tax with a credit. You're still "showing the income," which sometimes plays more nicely with other parts of the tax return.

If you've ever felt like exclusions are a magic trick ("the income disappears!"), the FTC is more like a receipt ("the income is there, and it was taxed over there, so adjust the bill accordingly"). For many expats, receipts are easier to defend.

A relatable FTC story: the accountant's idea of romance

Imagine two friends, both earning the same salary abroad.

Friend A lives in a low-tax jurisdiction and pays a small amount of local income tax. The IRS looks at Friend A's return and basically says, "You've paid some tax abroad; thanks for the update. You still owe us the rest."

Friend B lives in a higher-tax country. Friend B pays local income tax that's roughly comparable to—or higher than—what the IRS would charge on that same income. The IRS does its calculation, then applies the FTC, and the U.S. tax due on that slice of income often collapses.

Neither friend did anything sneaky. The tax code is simply acknowledging a world where Americans can live elsewhere and still be taxable at home. The FTC is the tool that keeps that from turning into a permanent two-cashier shakedown.

The deeper point: whether the FTC "covers" your U.S. income tax is not a personality trait. It's math driven by where you live, what you earn, and how that country taxes it.

The first planning question worth asking

Forget the forms for a moment. The first useful planning question is wonderfully blunt:

> Is my effective income tax rate abroad likely higher than my U.S. effective rate on the same income?

If yes, the FTC is often the main event. If no, the FTC still matters, but it may not be enough on its own.

This question also pushes you toward reality-based decisions. People sometimes choose a strategy because it *sounds* like what expats do—"I heard you just exclude everything" or "I heard you always take the credit." The truth is more personal and more pragmatic. You don't choose between tools based on expat folklore; you choose based on the actual tax weight in the country where you're building your life.

The FTC has a matching rule: you don't get credit for taxes tied to excluded income

Here's one of the strictest guardrails in expat taxation: you can't use the same dollar of income to generate two different kinds of relief.

If income is excluded under the FEIE (and/or the housing exclusion), you can't also claim the FTC for the overseas income taxes tied to that excluded income. The logic is simple: if the IRS has already agreed not to tax that income, it won't also hand you a credit as if it did.

In practice, this creates a surprisingly common "expat own goal." Someone excludes income under the FEIE because it feels satisfying to make the number smaller, then later tries to claim the FTC on the same salary's foreign taxes because they paid a lot abroad. The rules force a reduction: the portion of overseas income tax that relates to excluded income gets carved out and becomes unusable as a credit.

The planning takeaway isn't "avoid the FEIE." It's "coordinate." Sometimes FEIE is still the right move. Sometimes FTC is. Sometimes a mix is optimal. But the tax code won't let you stack the benefits on the same income like you're applying coupons at a self-checkout that doesn't have a manager.

Why the FTC feels "cleaner" for long-term expat life

Many expats discover that the FTC is less about cleverness and more about staying out of trouble while living a normal life.

The FTC tends to match how other countries think about income tax: you earn locally, you pay locally, you report globally. Your U.S. return becomes a reconciliation rather than an alternate universe.

It can also feel more stable year to year. Exclusions have eligibility rules that care about days, travel, and where your tax home is. The FTC cares about something more mundane: did you have foreign-source income, and did you pay qualifying income tax on it?

That doesn't mean the FTC is frictionless—limitations and category rules can be surprisingly sharp—but the "story" is intuitive. A tax was paid to a real government on real income, and the IRS is being asked to recognize that payment to prevent the same income being taxed twice at full strength.

The subtle power move: the FTC keeps your income "in view"

A credit approach can keep your U.S. tax return looking more like a typical return: income reported, tax computed, tax reduced by credits. That "normal" structure has ripple effects.

For example, many tax calculations and phaseouts in the U.S. system are built around adjusted gross income and taxable income. Excluding income can change those numbers in ways that are sometimes helpful, sometimes not. The FTC doesn't remove the income; it offsets the tax. That distinction can matter for households that care about how other parts of the return behave.

This is one reason expats in high-tax countries often default to FTC thinking. If the overseas income tax already does most of the heavy lifting, the FTC can eliminate double taxation without rewriting the shape of your U.S. return.

The paperwork reality (without the paper cut)

Most people claim the FTC using Form 1116. Think of it less as a monster form and more as a sorting and matching exercise: identify the income, identify the related overseas income taxes, and compute how much credit can be used against U.S. tax.

Even if you eventually hand the job to a preparer, understanding that basic workflow protects you from expensive misunderstandings. You'll know what to ask:

- "Are we claiming these taxes as a credit or a deduction?"
- "Are any of these taxes tied to income we excluded?"
- "Does my country's tax year line up with the U.S. year, or are we dealing with timing issues?"

Those questions don't require you to memorize line numbers. They do require you to understand what the FTC is trying to do: prevent double taxation *without* accidentally turning foreign taxes into a tool for wiping out U.S. tax on income that wasn't foreign in the first place.

A quick gut-check: why your coworker's outcome may not apply to you

Expats love comparing notes. It's comforting. It's also dangerous.

Two people can live in the same country and have completely different FTC outcomes because of:

- different income types (salary vs dividends vs self-employment),
- different effective tax rates (deductions, family status, special expat regimes),
- different sourcing facts (where workdays happened, remote work arrangements),
- different timing (withholding versus final assessments).

So if a coworker says, "I owe nothing to the IRS because of the credit," treat it like hearing someone say, "My rent is only $1,200." Interesting. Possibly encouraging. Not transferable without details.

The FTC mindset: pay once, report twice, suffer once

Living abroad as a U.S. taxpayer has an unavoidable rhythm: you often report the same income to two authorities. The FTC is what makes that rhythm financially survivable for millions of people. It doesn't make the IRS disappear. It makes the math fairer.

If you want a simple way to know whether the FTC should be your first instinct, look at your annual income tax burden where you live now. If it already feels heavy, the FTC may be your best friend—quietly taking the edge off the U.S. bill without requiring your life to contort around exclusions. If it feels light, the FTC still helps, but it won't carry the whole load.

Either way, the practical promise stays the same: qualifying income taxes paid abroad can reduce your U.S. income tax *dollar for dollar*. And once you internalize that, expat tax planning stops being mystical and starts being mathematical—in the best possible way.

4.2 Limitation Rules, Income Baskets, and Why Sourcing Matters

The Foreign Tax Credit would be hilariously abusable if it worked like a universal gift card: pay a high levy somewhere, then use it to erase whatever you owe the IRS on anything. The U.S. government is many things, but it is not a fan of tradable coupons. So the FTC comes with guardrails that feel finicky until you see the policy behind them.

The policy is simple: the credit is meant to prevent *double* taxation, not to subsidize your U.S.-source life. That's why the FTC is limited to the portion of U.S. tax that's tied to *foreign-source taxable income*. Not foreign-source *gross* income. Not "income that had a passport stamp." Taxable income—after the deductions that get assigned to it. That one word, *taxable,* is where a lot of surprises are born.

Once you accept that the IRS is trying to match things—this income with that tax, this category with that category—the rest of the FTC rules stop feeling like random hoops and start feeling like accounting with a very stubborn referee.

The FTC limitation: why the IRS won't let you wipe out everything

Start with the limitation concept in everyday terms: the IRS asks, "How much U.S. tax is attributable to your foreign-source taxable income?" That number is your *maximum* FTC for the year (with more nuance later, but keep the picture crisp). If you paid more qualifying overseas income tax than that maximum, the extra doesn't vanish, but it also can't bulldoze your U.S. tax on U.S.-source income.

This answers a common emotional question: "I paid a ton of tax overseas—why do I still owe the IRS?" Because the IRS is not impressed by the *amount* you paid overseas. It cares whether the U.S. tax you're trying to offset is actually connected to foreign-source taxable income, and whether you're offsetting it with credits from the right category of income.

A quick example with rounded numbers:

- You have $200,000 of total taxable income.
- $150,000 of that is foreign-source taxable income.
- Your total U.S. income tax on the return comes out to $40,000.

Very roughly, your FTC "ceiling" is the portion tied to the foreign-source taxable income: $40,000 × ($150,000 / $200,000) = $30,000. If you paid $35,000 of qualifying overseas income tax, you don't get to erase the remaining $10,000 of U.S. tax that's attributable to U.S.-source taxable income. The limit is doing its job.

That's not cruelty; it's the design preventing a particular kind of mischief: using high levies on foreign dividends, for example, to eliminate U.S. tax on U.S.-based consulting income. The FTC is not supposed to let one category of income buy forgiveness for a completely different category.

Form 1116, stripped of mystique: sorting, matching, capping

People fear Form 1116 the way they fear a complicated espresso machine: too many parts, too many ways to do it wrong, and a vague sense that something will explode if you press the wrong